Leaving 6 Figures

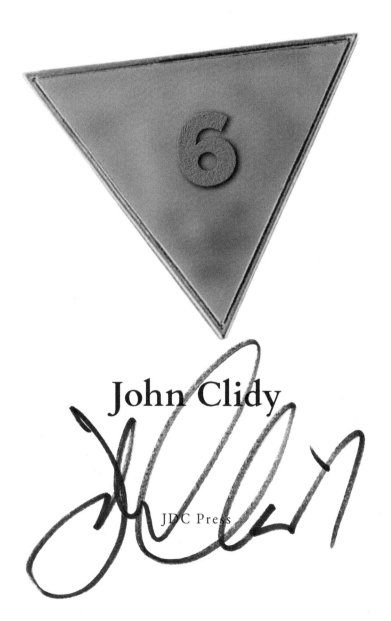

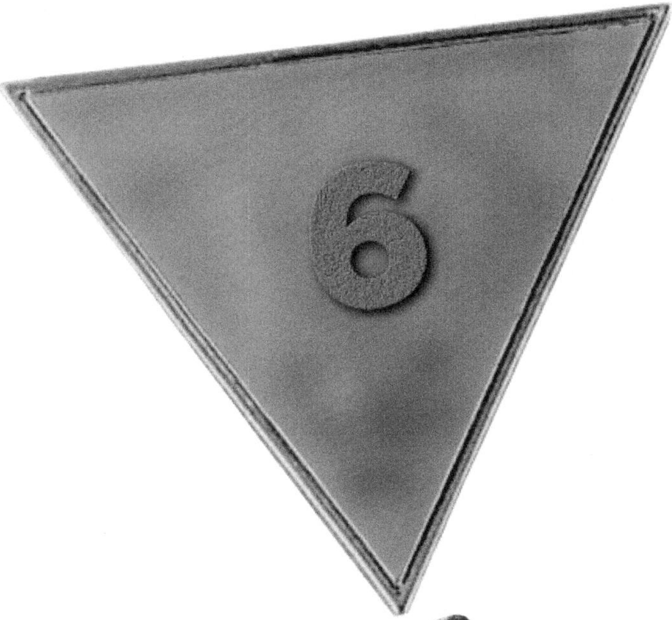

John Clidy

JDC Press

JDC Press, Sewell New Jersey

Library of Congress Control Number: 2020903743

Leaving 6 Figures / John Clidy -JDC Press- 1st ed.

LCC: 2020903743

ISBN 978-1-7346047-0-2

Contents

Dedication

Thanks Dad, Mom, Andrea,
Milana, Sienna, Natalia, and John Howard.

Dad, Cal Jada, I miss you.
I hope you are proud that I finally finished the book!

Here ya go! This book is for each one of you
and countless others who have made a mark in my life.

It Begins with Family

Instilling worthy character in a child is a challenge every parent understands. Who the youngster becomes, the person he or she grows into, is colored by their experiences from their first moments of consciousness and awareness. Does it matter if a person starts with a little then turns it into a lot? Some would say no. I say yes. Because that's me.

I started with a little. I've made it into a lot. My parents had limited education. My dad graduated the eighth grade. Mom received her high school diploma. There was no silver-spoon upbringing in our family. We were working-class. We fought every day to earn a living. Our family was provided for through bone-breaking effort and stubborn commitment to a strong work-ethic.

I appreciate every bit of help that got me to where I am today as a human being, not just a businessman. I do not take all the credit for my success. Writing this book is possible because of my Mom and Dad's support over the years.

I am certain I would not be the man I am without my incredible wife by my side. Andrea is special! Our remarkable children make our family complete.

John Clidy

Foreword

Mo Anderson

What a privilege it has been for me to know John Clidy. I have deep respect and admiration for him as a colleague, as a leader, as a husband and father, and as a former first responder on his state police force.

John's journey has not been a bee line toward success. He has overcome challenges and momentary setbacks along the way. He has learned that a dream career is not necessarily a precursor to happiness. In fact, as he shares in Leaving 6 Figures, sometimes one must take the road less traveled away from one career choice to discover true happiness down another path.

John's life experiences in dual careers, building passive income through investment, and the right mindset helped him to arrive at the heart of his message written here: *Recognize when it's time to leave and have the courage to embrace that change.* Status quo can lead to a stagnant life where growth is impossible. So, the question is: Are you doing what you love? Undoubtedly, all who invest their time in reading about John's journey will find nuggets of inspiration and encouragement to create a bigger vision for their lives in their own areas of passion. I personally love to teach others, there can be no vision without passion.

John Clidy has certainly found his passion and cast a vision by endeavoring to write this book. For that I am both grateful and so proud of him. May all who read Leaving 6 Figures find courage to take their own uncharted path.

About Mo Anderson

The youngest of five, born to tenant farmers in rural Oklahoma, Mo Anderson was the first in her family to earn a college degree. She taught music in the public schools before entering the world of real estate. Her first Century 21 franchise quickly rose to the third highest producing out of 7,500 locations in North America. She served on the Oklahoma Real Estate Commission, including two terms as chairman.

She convinced Keller Williams Realty Co-founder, Gary Keller, to expand his franchise company outside of Texas. Anderson became the regional owner for Keller Williams Realty Oklahoma. In 1995, Mo became the first CEO and co-owner of Keller Williams Realty International. The Company is now the number one Real Estate Franchise company in the world in size, units, and volume. She currently serves as Vice Chairman of the Board.

Deemed one of America's top 25 Influential Thought Leaders by REALTOR magazine and One of Real Estates Most Influential People, Anderson continues to cultivate the firm's culture, inspiring more than 180,000 agents in 33 countries to maintain high standards of character.

A member of the OK Hall of Fame (class of 2018), Mo is the author of *A Joy-filled Life: Lessons from a Tenant Farmer's Daughter Who Became a CEO*, and she launched MoAnderson.com, an online mentoring community.

Anderson's greatest legacy will be her philanthropic giving. Her local community, charitable organizations, and ministries around the world have been richly blessed by her belief that the higher purpose of business is to give, care and share.

INTRODUCTION

Reality Has Meaning

ARE YOU WORKING AT A JOB OR IN A CAREER that you don't love? Has this been your reality for years? Have you hated what you do? Do you, year after year, feel increasingly trapped in the wrong job?

I was that person who did not love what I did. It took 17 years after I decided I wanted to leave before I took the leap. When I did, I walked away from a guaranteed government pension.

Yes. You read that right.

I left a state pension on the table. Only three years shy of vesting the pension, I tendered my resignation.

Finally, fully aware, certain in my heart it was the right decision, I stepped into a life of which I had dreamed. I entered the life I knew would become possible when I took that leap of faith.

Why did it take so long? Waiting for 17 years easily cost me millions. I knew, as every year passed, that I was giving up huge potential earnings.

Why? It was fear. I was a cop, so you know that admitting to fear is not always easy. Fear. Worry about losing the false security of a job. Fear of the unknown. Doubt that I could make it happen even though I clearly saw the way forward.

Simple fear clouded my mind. Uncertainty kept me living a lie for the last nine years of my career as a NJ State Trooper.

In this book, I share stories from my life. We will relive events that happened during my long journey from a small-town, average student athlete to become a leader of leaders who owns multiple companies across three states. The stories that define who I am today show you the way to who you could be tomorrow.

This journey was marked by pork chop grease fights, dead bodies, drug deals, big money losses, big money gains, business failures, and business successes. The complexities of being a state trooper who was simultaneously a top real estate agent and investor taught me tons of lessons.

These are the lessons I will share to show you how an average person rose from being a hard-working middle-class citizen to become a multi-millionaire real estate mogul who juggles family dynamics and multiple careers! Today, I run one of the largest regions in Keller Williams with almost 10,000 agents across three states and 49 market centers.

In the stories I tell, in the experiences I share, it is my hope that you find the courage to step onto your own path, to change your journey.

Mixing with the stories will be discussion along with action steps and suggestions to assess your current situation to determine where you stand. Are you wishing for a guide to light your walk into a new life? Are you ready to leave your comfortable pension career or long-term job? Maybe you are a cop, like I was, or a schoolteacher, nurse, firefighter, corrections officer—you name the profession! Are you scared to death to leave because of your own laundry list of reasons?

How to achieve balance is easily the most important lesson I will share with you. This is the one lesson that, while achievable, will never be finished. Being the best husband, dad, son, friend, and partner is more important than all else!

Are you doing what you WANT to do in life? If not, what's stopping you? We only get one life, why not enjoy it? Let's make sure you live your life by design! You should not be stuck in a life where you wake up every morning dreading the day.

It's journey time. We are doers. Let's Go! Join me this time on the journey. I will show you the way to your success.

Section 1

The State Police

Chapter One

Lottery Wins Are Not Always Jackpots

IT WAS MOTHER'S DAY, MAY 19, 1997. *I woke at 2:30,* AM *instantly wide awake, a myriad of emotions—eager, scared, concerned, excited—spinning through me.*

I had packed and repacked and organized throughout the weekend. I packed every item on the list as per instructions, including. t-shirts, underwear, boots, sneakers, raincoats, socks, shoeshine, and even a certain type of shoe. It was over

100 pounds of stuff that had to fit in one bag. Most candidates reported with a duffel bag full of the required articles.

Oh, we also had to be bald. Yes, clean-shaven head bald! AND in a suit. AND they clearly stated that I had better be there an hour early.

I was to report at 6 AM (meaning 5 AM) to Sea Girt, about an hour and 45-minute drive from my home in Williamstown, NJ. I arrived at 4:50 AM to be greeted at the gate by large, intimidating troopers. Menacing. Not nice at all. Commands were curt, shouted as if volume lent power to the words.

"Drive up and park in the designated area."

"You will see troopers ahead directing you to park."

"GO!"

"GO!"

"Get out of here!"

I was told to stay in the car until further notice. I joined a lot full of candidates also seated in their parked cars. Around 6:05 AM, troopers ordered us out of the cars. We stood at attention with bag in hand for nearly 45 minutes in full sun on a hot day, fully dressed in a suit and tie. Candidates were sweating profusely. Several passed out. They were ordered to leave. I think seven candidates left within the first hour.

I remember wondering if I had lost my mind. What had possessed me to volunteer for this? At the same time, I acknowledged the confidence boost it was to get through the first hurdle. I was finally on my way.

IN 1994, I WAS FRESH OUT OF COLLEGE, full of optimism, and looking to start a career. Recruiters had been to the college campus for every kind of career you might imagine. The New Jersey State Police (NJSP), at the time I applied to become a trooper, was the most decorated law enforcement organization in the country. Everything was about excellence. That impressed me. I was strongly attracted to becoming a state trooper. I still value and respect the organization, even though it has changed.

The NJSP offered a promising career that included a solid income with great opportunities to advance, all of which was important to me. I liked the prestige of *The Outfit* (a label we used to describe the state police). There's no doubt that the image and reputation of the state police strongly influenced my decision to apply for admission to the 116th NJSP class.

Peer pressure could also have been a factor, as several of my teammates from Montclair State football also applied. We thought it would be easy. After all, we were *Alpha Males* ready for any challenge.

I never made it past the written phase for the 116th. Neither did any of my college football buddies. A year later I received a call telling me that my test scores were still good and asking, "Did I want to apply for the 117th NJSP class?"

It felt like I won the lottery. They came back to ask me to apply again. 10,000 people applied. They accepted only a few hundred candidates. Even fewer would make it through the training process to become a New Jersey State Trooper.

This time, I made it through the written, oral, psychological, physical fitness, and medical phases of the application process this time.

Then they started on the background check.

What an experience that was! I gave three references. Investigators went three-deep on each reference. In all, they contacted nine references. In addition, I opened my school records to them, from kindergarten through college, as well as military and law enforcement service at any level. The background interviews included meeting with my neighbors from when I was a child and where I currently lived, in addition to interviewing my entire immediate family.

It was an intense experience, as it should be! State Troopers have a huge responsibility and impressive power. I've always tried to live up to the expectations and image of the outfit.

There have been many books published about the New Jersey State Police. I applied to join a world class organization. Colonel Herbert Norman Schwarzkopf was the first Superintendent back in 1921. Colonel Schwarzkopf's son was the famous Stormin' Norman of the Gulf War.

I valued being a part of the outfit's tradition, especially at the start of my career. It seemed like every possible avenue of support was offered to guide a trooper to be the best.

At last I received word to report to *The Academy* for training. The Academy was an adjustment for me because it was paramilitary; a way of life I had never been exposed to. They scheduled me for six months of grueling training, in the dead of summer, on the beach in Sea Girt, NJ. I would be returning home on weekends then required to report at 6 AM every Monday morning. Friday's dismissal would be whatever time suited the Commandant on that day.

I really had no idea what I was getting into, even though by this time I had heard a few hell stories. Some claimed it was harder than Marine boot camp. That first day, standing in the parking lot holding my 100-pound packed duffel bag, I believed every horror story I'd been told.

I remember one Monday morning they did a vehicle inspection as we were coming onto the campus. I was told to place my hands on the steering wheel and wait my turn. I saw guys scrambling to clean up or maybe hide things, but I sat tight. I did as ordered.

Later we heard that they kicked three candidates out after the car inspection! One guy was booted for having marijuana seeds in an ashtray. Two others had open containers or empty alcohol containers in their vehicles. Crazy, right?

The Academy was grueling mentally and physically. They pushed us to the limit daily. We were held to an impossibly high standard. My quarters had to be kept always tidy. We had military drills, schoolwork, physical fitness, self-defense, shooting, guard duty, and lessons that challenged the human spirit.

Instructors stayed on our backs continuously. They wanted to break us. Some did break. I never worried about being broken mentally.

I worried about my knees, though. I blew out both knees playing college football. Many nights I thought those surgically repaired knees would be my breaking point. We ran every day. It tested every inch of my physical limitations and mental resolve to keep going when my knee was the size of a grapefruit. Ice and Advil became my dear friends.

I would sneak an ice pack in when I knew I'd be sitting for a long class. A few instructors were no-nonsense. They gave me a hard time about icing my knee, making me clean up any water puddle I created from the ice that melted, then I had to run laps around the building!

I did have one unusual physical challenge, aside from my knees. We had to pass a lifeguard certification that included treading water for a long time. Jersey is a coastal state bordered by an ocean. Aquatic lifesaving knowledge was required. Of course, it wasn't enough to just float in a pool. They had to up the game. They added ice to the water, or at least it felt like it. We had to tread water for a long time in freezing water at the YMCA pool in Asbury Park.

We lost a few guys there. I also remember losing guys for not being honest about their background, for injuries during training, or who tapped out because they were broken. We started with 165 candidates; 112 graduated.

I came into the academy in the best physical shape of my life at 230 pounds. We had little sleep or food and were always being called to task. We had two to three minutes to eat, sometimes during hell week even less. I left the academy a different person.

Graduation Legacy

Near the end of my training that summer, I remember thinking, "I'm really going to make it! I will be a New Jersey State Trooper!"

Every day I envisioned wearing that electric blue and gold uniform. On October 3, 1997, my vision became real. It was a proud moment when I received my badge from the Colonel and the Governor of NJ. Suddenly every moment of the challenges, obstacles, and stress of living through six months of mental anguish was worthwhile.

Graduation was cool. I was a decent boxer. It was an honor to be asked to give a boxing demonstration as part of the graduation ceremonies.

Tradition had that each graduating class would add something of value to the campus. For my graduation class, my brother Joey built the Physical Fitness Stand (AKA the PT Stand) which was like a stage where one candidate performed an exercise. Those in the audience also performed the exercise, following the lead of the candidate on stage. All NJ State Troopers know about the PT stand. The physical fitness demonstration is usually comprised of pushups, jumping jacks, and leg raises. It's been known to go on for 30 minutes straight at times.

The stand Joey built included a name plate which stated, "Dedicated from the 117th NJSP class." It's pretty cool that my little brother created something that was used for many state police classes after mine.

Woodbine, Red Lion, and Bridgeton

Graduating from the academy is not the end of a trooper's learning. It takes 18 months on the job before new grads (boots, recruits, rookies, we answered to whatever they wanted to call us) are vested troopers. During that time, I spent six months rotating through three stations, all outside my home territory, where I lived.

My first station was in Woodbine, an hour and 15-minute drive one way from my home. They still required me to get there an hour early!

This assignment was filled as much with learning as it was an initiation. New recruits are expected to do chores. We got to wash cars, do the dishes left by the prior squad shift, and clean up the station, to name a few of the popular jobs relegated to the new guy.

What kind of lesson did I learn as the new trooper? To pay the dues required to learn the job. I also learned when to let things roll off my back and move on. Perhaps the most important lesson from those days was to remember to pay it back and pay it forward.

Back then, our shifts ran 10 hours, overlapped to spread across the 24-hour day. We were typically assigned one of these 10-hour shifts: 6AM-4PM, 12PM-10PM, or 9PM-7AM, which was called *midnights.* I started on midnights. I loved the 10-hour shift. I hated when we went to 12-hour shifts.

By today's standards, we had archaic tools. No cameras or computers in the car. We used typewriters, yellow out, and white out.

After six months in Woodbine, they reassigned me to Red Lion. We worked overtime like crazy in Red Lion. They were exceptionally short on manpower at the time. Being required to work back-to-back shifts was common.

I recall one night there was a get together to celebrate some guy's transfer. We had a trooper on our squad who unfortunately never made it home that night. He was tired from working and fell asleep behind the wheel. It was not long after, I think, that they changed the policy to restrict the number of hours a trooper could work overtime on back-to-back shifts.

Sometimes You Feel Like a Cop

When I transferred to Bridgeton barracks two months later, it was like going back in time. They had a group of guys in that station who acted like enforcers. They called themselves Phantoms, or something like that. I never figured out what their name meant, but I did earn my own nickname while there.

> *By this time, four months after graduation, I had regained most of the weight I lost while at the academy. At nearly 250 pounds, I was one of the bigger guys. Like most troopers, I thought my stuff didn't stink. I resented doing anybody else's dishes. The chores got old really fast for me. I started to 'accidentally' forget lunch orders so the guys would not ask me to do that again.*
>
> *A few troopers took exception to my attitude. One day I came in to find my work mailbox was full of salt. Yes. Salt.*
>
> *I snapped. I slammed the salt and all my paperwork all over the floor and said, "Whoever did it, clean this shit up!"*
>
> *After I calmed down a bit, a Sergeant I respected told me to just clean it up. He said that he would get them to chill. From then on, they called me Salty. (Salty was the name given to a trooper who acted out of line, usually a rookie or boot like me got that label)*
>
> *I think they just wanted me to act more like a rookie. I guess I was full of myself. I got their message. Looking back, I believe I could have found a better way to deliver my message, too. That's a lesson I learned well.*

It was in Bridgeton that I began to think of myself as a trooper. It was here I saw my first suicide victim, experienced the amazing pork chop grease fight, witnessed many assaults, and experienced fatal accident victims.

One of the first autopsies I saw struck closer to home than I expected. I have never been bothered being around death. In fact, I thought something was wrong after my first homicide because it really did not bother me.

This autopsy was different. The victim was a 17-year-old boy who died in a car accident. At that time, my little brother, Joey was 17, which may explain why this experience has stuck with me strongly after all these years. Somehow, I associated my brother with that unfortunate teen. That sparked my emotions. Fortunately, I was okay during the autopsy. It was when I walked back to my trooper car that the emotion hit me. My brother, who is nine years younger than me, could have been lying on that cold, metal table.

To this day I don't believe I have ever told Joey this story. Nor have I spoken much about why that autopsy had such a strong impact on me. Family is important. They are why we do what we do and who we least want to disappoint in life.

The Pork Chop Grease Fight

Bridgeton was also the location for the pork chop grease fight. I'll bet there are troopers still talking about that call. It was memorable.

We arrived in the Sea Brook village complex, which was a holocaust survivor's community turned into low income government housing. To say the housing units were small was an understatement. They called us in for a domestic dispute. As soon as my partner and I arrived, we heard people shouting, pain evident in their screams. We smelled an odd odor that grew more potent as we approached the small row home.

I shouted as we entered, "NJSP!"

Right away I saw two small children in the oppressively hot home. The kids were alone in the living room with no adult supervision. Both appeared to be two or three years old. They were unkempt and weighted down with dirty diapers.

The odd smell that caused our noses to wrinkle up in distaste when we were outside the house, struck like a blow from a fist as we entered the room.

Grease. Cooking meat. Used baby diapers.

Indescribable.

You had to be there.

My shouted identification could not have been heard over the loud yelling coming from further inside the building. We pulled out our guns. Cautiously, we entered the kitchen to see something I will never forget.

Two people, highly intoxicated or on drugs, screamed at each other as they flung hot pork chop grease across the room at each other.

Yes! Sizzling, boiling, fryer-hot pork chop grease.

It covered everything and everybody in the room. There were chunks of burned skin falling off their bodies. The stench of booze, frying grease, and crispy human skin was unbearable. In this kitchen, the odd smell turned into a gag-inducing, rancid odor that cut through every attempt to NOT smell it.

Amid our own choking gags, we barked out orders for them to stop then got the situation under control while somehow managing not to touch either of them. We called for EMT support. Both were charged then released to hospital care.

It was one experience I truly will never forget.

We also called the DYFS for the children. Those poor kids. Maybe the only saving grace from that night is that they were too young to remember any of it.

Undercover in North Jersey

I also was part of some big undercover operations in North Jersey. Let me tell you, undercover is a whole different kind of law enforcement. I recall one assignment that was a big, dangerous operation. The undercover job was for the ABC

(Alcoholic Beverage Control) Unit. It was organized as a joint task force with the FBI and several local law enforcement departments.

The operation focused on the Crystal Club Lounge, which was a pizza shop front with a gentleman's go-go bar underneath. The bouncers for the bar were mostly members of a nationally known gang, which made sense since the whole operation was a gang-run business.

The gang was harboring underage girls and running them as prostitutes. A lot of these girls were runaways from bad homes or had no families. They were caught up in the gang life with no way out.

Gang members heavily secured the entrance to the bar. There was one way in and one way out and no way to get a gun inside. A few times, they questioned me at the door, "You a cop? I never seen you around."

I got lucky on that. One of my teammates from college football worked security for the club. He vouched for me. He did not know I was a state trooper. I do not think he was a gang member, just a large man (he weighed over 350 pounds), who worked in security.

It was bizarre inside. Sex acts and drug deals occurred right in front of my eyes. I went in armed with a blue jean jacket (they were the style back in the day) that had a camera on the button. It didn't take long to find out that the camera feed did not work in the club's basement. My partner and I were stranded with no eyes from the outside and no guns. At least I always had one other officer undercover inside the establishment with me.

We would hang around the neighborhood prior to going inside of the club. The idea was to fit in. We would buy a 40-ounce malt liquor then play the role (that's what we called it). Then we'd go inside to continue our undercover investigation.

Today I think it's crazy that I (or anybody) walked into that situation by choice, with no weapons and our only backup a lone partner armed exactly the same.

I never worried about it; I was fearless then.

After a few months of gathering evidence, word came down that we were going to 'hit' the place. The plan was for me and my partner to go in ahead of the raid. We'd be inside already and get 'caught' during the raid. Then we'd get locked up with everyone else to protect our cover.

To make a long story short, someone tipped them off. Come raid time, none of the juveniles being exploited were there, nor was the head of the gang's females (who was bartending) or any of the other leaders for the gang. We grabbed plenty of guns, drugs, and suspects with outstanding warrants, but not the gang leaders we intended to arrest or the juveniles we hoped to rescue.

I was a young, single male, still in the 'honeymoon' phase of my time as a trooper. It was a great time for me to go undercover. I respect those who successfully make a career of undercover work. It's important work and necessary. It's also a job I would NOT take on today.

Is Waiting Worth Your Life?

Not long after graduating from the academy, I bought a 'fixer upper' in my hometown to live in. I needed a place to live as well as something to do during my off time. My fixer upper turned out to be more than I bargained for since it led me directly into my true calling.

I had a lot to learn and was fortunate to find the first broker I worked with early in my career. He owned tons of properties in my hometown. I wanted to follow his lead on investing, so when another real estate agent offered me a house deal, I took him up on the offer. The agent thought few people wanted to buy in Camden and he wanted out of the deal. I thought that, since the house was a duplex and the rental market was on fire, there was money to be made by the right person. That right person was me. I flipped the house. In 30 days, I made 60k.

I was hooked on real estate after my first real deal because I made real money.

Mindset Flip

That was the start of my investing business. I no longer needed banks to buy houses! It brought about a paradigm shift in my mindset from cop to real estate mogul.

I did not give up the police. It was three years of part-time real estate dabbling before I believed in the potential to earn huge money. Then for 17 years, I did both. As I drove around being a trooper, I looked at homes to buy and helped clients.

Did I ever mix business with pleasure? Sure. I won't lie about it. I did sometimes meet a client or attend a settlement while 'on the job'. I truly performed in BOTH careers at a high level—at least in the early days. They call it dual career now. I think I was managing a triple career, if there was such a thing—trooper, realtor, and investor.

Flipping my mindset from cop to business owner happened kind of fast. Going undercover didn't really impact this, although it opened my eyes to just how dangerous the career I'd chosen could be. One especially dangerous incident stands out to me—it was the day I realized I would be killed if I did not leave the state police.

> *I was working with the Camden Shoot team. We were looking for a murder suspect. At the time, Camden, NJ was the #1, most dangerous city in the country. We were downtown, near Rutgers University, walking through a neighborhood of row houses, strategically searching for the criminal suspect. I was part of a team of three troopers and four Camden city and county detectives.*
>
> *The suspect was armed. We did not have a SWAT team, so*

we were going in protected by our wits and bullet-proof vests. We were a small team of men carrying guns and a few rifles searching for a dangerous suspect known to be in the area.

As we approached the target house, I remember noticing how nice the neighborhood looked. The house was in an historic area. The property presented well from outside with an attractive brick facade.

Think about where my head was! Instead of worrying about the armed murder suspect who could shoot me at any moment, I was assessing houses!

We entered the target house, uncertain if the suspect was there or not. We walked with guns drawn, in imminent danger. We operated in a high alert state. We were never sure what was ahead, or behind for that matter.

Amid this tense situation, I stopped to look through a pile of unopened letters. One guy asked, "What are you doing?"

Without thinking I said, "I see foreclosure notices. I could buy this at the sheriff sale. It's a nice house, don't you think? Right next to Rutgers University, so a good investment."

He made a huffing sound and shook his head, then said, "You're crazy. Let's focus on getting out of here alive, Realtor Clidy... I mean, Trooper Clidy."

Just like that I earned a name in the outfit as *The Realtor*. That was when I knew I was on short time with the NJ State Police. In my heart, even though it was years before I would leave, that was the day a balance shifted. My mindset crossed the line toward businessman and away from trooper. Later, I checked the sheriff sales to find the property. I never did end up purchasing the home.

Being on the job in Camden was when I first felt like a realtor. I was flipping my mindset along with the houses. Some thought I was flipping out of my mind. I never worried about how dangerous it was to be a cop in Camden when the crime rate was so high—I worried about my deals.

Yes, I knew I would get myself killed if I did not choose between two intense careers. How to choose seemed obvious. Only one of those careers, if I was complacent at the wrong time, could get me killed. It was a no-brainer to give up law enforcement. But not quite yet.

Life Lesson: Timing

Those early days becoming a seasoned trooper taught me skills and principles that I honor to this day. The stories in this book share a common theme—recognizing the lessons life teaches. AND taking the lesson a step further to act upon the inspiration or knowledge gained.

Together we will pause at the end of each chapter to reflect on the lesson in your own life that can be used in a meaningful way—by you.

Whenever we present a Life Lesson, we will include space to write answers to the questions we pose. This book is a **WOOK** (a **W**orkb**OOK**) for you to use as a resource and energy dial when you need it!

My intention with this book is to guide you in creating your own plan to be happy. Let's create a plan that covers all the holes in our life. Use this book as a jumping off point to build a legacy for you and your family.

Whether you prefer to write your answers separately or write in the book, we recommend you do pause and write your response. We reference those answers as you progress through the lessons and again when you create your **Leaving 6 Figures Take Action Plan**.

LET'S THINK ABOUT THIS...

1. Have you asked yourself, "Is this the job I want for the rest of my life?"

2. Are you like I was, in a job where you could get hurt if your mindset is not right? Maybe it's not about danger with you. Your peril could be from depression, divorce, a difficult situation with family or even a crisis of conscience or legal issue. Truly, take time to reevaluate things ASAP before you or somebody gets hurt.

3. Have you ever thought about comparing your job to buying a house? Most people first buy a starter home, understanding that they will not be there forever. Are you in a starter job?

4. In terms of your job what stage are you in? Are there issues now with your job that were not there at the beginning? Often, we feel trapped as life happens. Almost overnight, we have families and debt. Fear of being without the 'security' of the job looms heavily over our heads. Are you feeling trapped? Disappointed? Bored? Challenged? Journal about it. Use the space in the book or use a separate notebook.

5. Here's a crazy fact: winning the lottery does not erase problems. Happiness is not solely based on having money. Do you know what makes you happy? Reflect on your why. What do you believe is your purpose in life?

6. The stories shared in this chapter are from the early days of my life as a state trooper. I have hundreds more. I chose these to demonstrate the lessons of life that came to me after these experiences. Were you able to draw an analogy in your own life in reading these shared stories? What lesson do you believe you've taken away from this chapter?

7. Still thinking about the stories I've shared thus far and the points we've touched on. Is there an action you will take in your life to make a change, based on this lesson?

"It doesn't matter where you start. It matters where you finish."

T. D. Jakes, pastor, author and filmmaker

This was something my father said to me often. I don't know if he knew it as a quote from T. D. Jakes, but he knew it as a reality of life. It was a lesson he wanted me to embrace.

Unfortunately, in his younger years my dad became a convicted felon. A positive part of this experience was that he was in prison with the famous Rueben Hurricane Carter. (Will Smith played Carter when they made a movie about his life.)

My dad fought Hurricane in prison. It was an organized boxing match in the Trenton State Penitentiary. I don't remember my dad ever saying who won the fight. I say Cal Jada won! (Cal Jada was my dad's boxing name.)

My dad was an aspiring boxer prior to getting into trouble in the mid-60s. Then he was an incredible citizen, loving family man, and successful businessman for five decades after serving his time.

I'm proud of him and what he accomplished, especially considering where he began.

CHAPTER TWO

Are You Doing What You Love?

WHILE I WAS A TROOPER, I ASKED myself this question a lot. I had a great job, one that many people wanted.

Did I truly want it?

Everyone told me it was a great job. It sure did come with perks. I could literally speed down the highway as a civilian or while working. I didn't wait in lines when I went to the shows, lounges, or night clubs. I had a free car that came with gas and insurance. Some even claimed I had a 'get out of jail free' card.

So, why didn't I love this great job? Why did I go to work at times sick to my stomach, feeling like I didn't belong?

I'm not sure if it was because of my success in real estate or truly that the state police was not my life passion. Either way, I had to do a lot of self-discovery to figure out what the heck was going on inside of me.

People envied me when I got the job as a trooper. To them, it really was a lottery win. I would hear stuff all the time like, "I tried to get that job. I did not make it." Or "My son wanted to be a NJ State Trooper."

It was a prestigious job in the eyes of the outside world. In 2001, I was a finalist for the *Trooper of the Year Award.* I received a yellow ribbon for my diligent, honorable patrol duty while on the Atlantic City Expressway. Yet, when I was a trooper, I didn't feel elite.

I don't think my fellow officers did either. A fair majority of Troopers were disgruntled. They were not happy with where they were; not getting promoted; had problems at home; were bullied or teased by their peers. The list of gripes was long. Being a state trooper came with high levels of job-related stress.

Did these troopers hate their jobs? Did I hate my job? Hate is a strong word. I can absolutely say that I had strong feelings. At times I did not want to be at work as a trooper. There were days I experienced an intense feeling of dread. That seemed to happen regularly around the time I was transferred to Atlantic City.

I realized then that, to my employers, I was badge #5573. I was a number, not John Clidy a person. I think the academy brainwashed us to forget that being a trooper is only a job. I was an employee of the ultimate business.

It could be a generational thing that I was taught government pensions are the best. I grew up beliving a government job to be the pinnacle of achievement. It was understood that you never leave a government job until you get the pension.

My dad loved what he did. He was good at it, even though he had to self-medicate with a drink at night then rub on icy hot for his sore muscles so he could go right back and do it again the next day. He did that for nearly 50 years!

People who love their jobs, like teachers, firefighters, and cops, are special people. They would do their jobs no matter how much it paid. That's how it should be. You should love what you do. Why wake up each day sick to your stomach, unsure why you are doing what you are doing?

Think about this: most people spend more time at work than they do with family, 40-80 hours a week. By the time you get home, eat dinner, and go to bed, there are maybe 20 hours a week to spend with family. That's not even considering the busy schedules the kids have, which means part of those 20 hours are spent in the car going to and from school, social events, and in a plethora of crazy busy weekend activity.

It's no wonder that a recent Gallup poll reported one-third of a workforce is fully engaged.

Are you an engaged worker whose performance and efficiency are at high levels? Do you have an emotional commitment to what you do? Is your energy and enthusiasm caught by other employees?

Or are you a disengaged worker who may have been actively engaged at one time? Perhaps you became disengaged because of a lack of career growth or promotion, or a perception of salary inequity. Have you come to dislike the job or distrust your manager or senior management?

Your job or career—what you do for a living and how you feel when at work—is important. So is working with people who also value their job. I have employees tell me they were made physically ill from the stress brought on by people they worked with (or for). These people liked their jobs but hated working with a particular person.

I worked with incredible people during my 17 years with the state police. For me, it was not the people. For me, it was the job itself. Every time I went to the shooting range or attended annual in-service trainings, I would look around and say to myself, "Man, I do not fit in here."

My mindset was not in alignment with what was going on in my environment. I started asking myself, "Is it me or them? Why do I feel like this?" I came to question why I continued. I worked in a dangerous job. I faced situations every day that could get me killed. It was not fair to my family or me to put myself in that position. I needed to be in it to win it, because my life truly depended on it.

I think I did, in some way, hate the job. I was appreciative of the opportunity. I valued the relationships created while I was there. Yet, as time went on, I grew farther away from the career I worked so hard to get. I came to realize I didn't want to work as a trooper any longer.

I think it might be like in a marriage or relationship when you grow out of love. When one person develops who they are and the other does not, they grow out of alignment or out of love. I think that is what happened to me. The job no longer was in alignment with my life or the goals I wanted to achieve.

What is it for you? Do you hate your job? Is it the job or is it a person or a situation? Both? Neither? You owe it to yourself to find out, then make a plan to change the situation.

Life Lesson: Transition

In 2013, Forbes magazine reported on a global poll conducted by Gallup saying that "work is more often a source of frustration than fulfillment for nearly 90% of the world's workers. The rate is slightly better in countries like the US, where only 70% of people hate their jobs. A staggering 94% of workers in China and Japan are not engaged."

Do you work in a company where a boss is a problem? Or maybe you developed a dislike for the job due to an individual? Do you feel that you've been treated poorly or unfairly and are fed up? There are countless reasons to stay and for most just as many reasons to make a change. It can be helpful to gauge your true commitment to your current situation. The questions below are similar to those asked by Gallup in their poll. You may find your answers provide insight into your level of engagement.

*There are no right or wrong answers to this short exercise. Compare the number of **True** responses you gave to the number of **False** responses. The higher the ratio of False responses, the more disengaged you may be as an employee.*

T F I know what is expected of me at work.

T F I have the tools I need to do my work right.

T F At work, I have the opportunity to do what I do best every day.

T F I receive recognition or praise for doing good work.

T F My supervisor, or someone at work, seems to care about me as a person.

T F There is someone at work who encourages my development.

T F At work, my opinions seem to count.

T F The mission or purpose of my company makes me feel my job is important.

T F My fellow employees are committed to doing quality work.

T F I have a best friend at work.

T F In the last six months, someone has talked to me about my progress.

T F This last year, I have had opportunities at work to learn and grow.

LET'S THINK ABOUT THIS...

1. Did the quiz above give you any insights about your current employment situation?

2. Do you hate your job? Gallup says 23% of global employees are actively disengaged and for all intents, hate their job. What do you hate about it? (Even if you don't hate the whole job, describe the parts you dislike.)

3. Could the situation improve? Is it a person or the actual job you hate?

4. Are you part of the problem?

5. Can you name one part of the job you like?

6. If you said YES to the first question and hate your job, give yourself a date by which time you will review your situation and remove yourself from the job you hate.

______________________ ______________________

Date **Initials**

Colonel Sanders went to more than 1,000 places trying to sell his chicken recipe before he found an interested buyer.

Thomas Edison tried almost 10,000 times before he succeeded in creating the electric light.

The original business plan for what became Federal Express was given a failing grade on Fred Smith's college exam. In the early days, FedEx employees would cash their pay checks at retail stores rather than banks. This took longer for the money to clear, thereby giving Fed Ex more time to cover their payroll.

The poet Robert Frost had his first poetry submissions to The Atlantic Monthly returned unwanted.

Sylvester Stallone was turned down a thousand times by agents. He was down to his last $600 before he found a company that would produce Rocky and keep him in the title role. The rest is history!

"Nothing can take the place of persistence.
Talent will not....
Genius will not....
Education will not....
Persistence, determination, and love are omnipotent."

~ Ray Kroc, Founder McDonalds Restaurants

SECTION 2

Dual Career

Chapter Three

Hard Work and Payoff

(Or Why I Got into Real Estate)

EVERY YEAR AT LEAST 100,000 PEOPLE get into the real estate industry. You can only imagine how often I am asked, "Why did you get into real estate?"

Let me ask you realtors out there, did you wake up as a 10-year-old and announce, "I am going to be a Realtor!"

The profession is more likely entered as a side job for extra money. Or as a plan for a career change, a new beginning. Or simply to leverage time with your family or to run away from the structure of living within banker hours. Real Estate has an easy barrier of entry. It offers high returns. These are the reasons why I think smart and savvy people get into real estate.

Me?

I backed into real estate as a business.

I purchased my first house right after I got out of the state police academy late in 1997. It was a small rancher in Williamstown, NJ.

As a trooper, I worked a 10-hour schedule, mostly nights. I had a lot of down time to fill. I purchased the home mostly so that I could fix it up, not to invest. I planned to live there. Or maybe rent it out if I got transferred. We had to rehab the entire kitchen, among other fixes, all of which took time and money.

Thank God for my handy little brother, Joey. At that time, he was around 17 years old. Joey's personality is like that of our Dad. As is often true, *Father* and *Youngest Son* were not on the same page. Joey moved in with me during his teenage years. I still have a strong sense of responsibility for my sibling, coming from that time when I was being more than a big brother to him. He turned out to be a really good human being, and a successful one, too.

We slept on the floor because I had no furniture yet as we rehabbed the home. We both spent every minute of our free time working on that house. Joey is one of the best I've seen with his hands, even at such a young age. After about five months we had the house ready to purchase furniture and turn it into a place for everyone to visit. I felt like an official homeowner.

Getting My Real Estate License

How did I turn a fixer upper into a million-dollar career? In the process of buying and rehabbing, I caught the bug and went after my real estate license. Everybody told me that it was nuts, but I knew that the idea wasn't as crazy as it looked on the surface.

Truth be told, I simply did not think that the realtor who sold me my first house told me everything I needed to know before I bought. Back then, I did not have a lot of money. Not being informed hurt me financially. The biggest omission was not being told to get an in-depth inspection. I paid for problems that would have been disclosed and negotiated, had I been properly informed.

I knew that I could do a better job. During that long first year of home ownership, I learned the hard way about what I did not know.

I decided lack of knowledge was something I could fix. No way was I letting my ignorance of real estate practices cost me time or money again. It was a surprising bonus when I saw how easily I could make extra money on the side by selling real estate.

At that time, I had no idea going after a casual side hustle (the term my cop friends used to describe moonlighting away from the police job) would lead me to a new career passion. Getting that real estate license re-scoped my entire life! It's truly remarkable how making a career in real estate has allowed me to touch so many other lives along the way.

A pair of old school brokers, in a small independent real estate office, took me on to learn the business. I was one of six agents in the office including the two owners. It was before computers. We used Multiple Listing System (MLS) catalogs to search and show homes. The listings were broken down by County. Going through those books was tedious.

I did not last long at this office. I came to learn that who you surround yourself with matters, in every setting.

Life Lesson: The Leadership Journey

I think during this part of my life, as I set out to master dual careers, I truly came to understand what I missed by not paying better attention in school. I began to read books. I took my education seriously. I learned to value knowledge and the experiences of others. I also learned how to leverage time. After all, reinventing the wheel is counterproductive.

What are you doing with your spare time? One lesson I hope you take from this book is to have passion for your work and the life journey you are on, perhaps even love what you do. Life is too short for anything else to make sense. Start small and grow.

In this book, we are reliving my path to leadership in hopes that by sharing experiences you will empower your choices, plans, and goals.

I learned about making what you read your own in a discussion with Gary Keller, CEO and Chairman of Keller Williams Realty. Now I am teaching it to you. When you read a book, if an idea resonates with you, make the concept your own. Internalize it. Then change it to reflect your point of view or perspective.

That's what I did after reading John Maxwells' *5 Levels of Leadership*. I created the acronym R.A.G.E.S.

R.A.G.E.S. defines the stages of the leadership journey, as I experience them. It's a model that I strive to follow as I grow as a leader; and as I grow other leaders in my world.

R.A.G.E.S

R stands for Role. It defines what's expected of you. It is essentially your job description.

A is about Alignment. As a leader, I understand how critically important it is that I am effective in sharing the vision. Everyone under my leadership must be aligned with my vision.

G stands for Growth. This is ongoing. Leaders continue to grow, personally and professionally. If you are not growing, you are dying.

E is about Evolving. Great leaders bring their team along on the growth journey. They help others to become leaders. It's not fun if you're the only one evolving in your organization. Bring your partners along on the ride.

S is the Summit. You are a leader among leaders when the leaders you helped to rise, pay it forward within their own organization to help others become leaders.

The summit is not the end, however. Leaders who reach the summit continually crest the next step, leading those coming behind to greater achievement. The leadership journey is not one taken alone. It is important that your team or staff evolve along with you. Bring as many of your leaders to the summit with you.

In applying the R.A.G.E.S. model, begin by defining the role you play now and the role you want to play, if they are different. Ensure that the Return on Investment (ROI) in that role is in alignment with your beliefs, goals, and expectations. Also ensure you're continuing to grow as a leader. In R.A.G.E.S., I found a guideline that helps me to help others. I use it to achieve my own goals too.

I like acronyms. **S.M.A.R.T** is another one of my favorites. The use of this acronym was coined in 1981 by consultant George T. Doran. He published a paper titled, *There's a S.M.A.R.T. Way to Write Management's Goals and Objectives.* I, like many people, believe that effective goals and objectives must incorporate all five elements of the SMART acronym Doran gave us:

Specific

Measurable

Achievable

Repeatable

Timely

This is a great example of a tool that can be adopted to fit your own unique situation. Not every goal or objective will meet the above criteria. The acronym is meant to focus your goal setting attention, allowing for targeted objectives. Creating tightly focused goals and objectives will improve your chances of success.

I use this acronym as I create goals for all my businesses. This practice has led to more consistency in hitting my goals. I'm sure it will do the same for you. Especially if you have no system currently.

Let's be SMART now and continue crafting your plan. Write your responses to the questions below. Remember we'll compile the lessons at the end to create your **Leaving 6 Figures Take Action Plan**.

LET'S THINK ABOUT THIS...

1. Are you learning based? What books are you reading? What podcasts are you listening to right now?

2. If none, let's pick a book to read or podcast to subscribe to. I love all of John Maxwell's Leadership Books. My favorite is *The 5 Levels of Leadership*. Also, Gary Keller best seller's: *Millionaire Real Estate Agent (MREA)* and *The One Thing*. My favorite Podcasts currently are: *Business Wars* and *Think Like a CEO*, with Gary Keller and Jay Papasan.

3. Do you have other interests in life? What are they? List them here.

4. How do those interests align with your current job? Or do they conflict?

5. Who are you hanging with? Are they good for you or bad for you? Married, Friends, Co-Workers, family? Are you around the right people to achieve your goals?

6. If you stop working, can your family make it? How does that make you feel if they would struggle? Do you want to be in control or will your job or a person have that control?

Steve Jobs was 21 when he and Steve Wozniak invented the Apple Computer. Until then, computers were a monstrous mass of vacuum tubes which filled whole rooms. Jobs and Wozniak offered their invention to Atari. Atari said no. They offered it to Hewlett Packard, Hewlett Packard also declined. It seemed only Jobs and Wozniak could see the possibilities. They set up business in a garage and the rest is history.

Jobs discovered that if his vision was to reach fruition, they needed greater management expertise. So, Jobs approached John Sculley, then President of PepsiCo. There was no reason why Sculley should leave a highly paid position in a world leading company to go work with a bunch of computer nerds in a fledgling industry.

Jobs asked Sculley this now classic question, "Do you want to spend the rest of your life selling sugared water or do you want a chance to change the world?"

Indeed, Jobs and Sculley did change the world.

"If you have a strong commitment to your goals and dreams, if you wake up every day with a passion to do your job, everything is possible."

~ Chantal Petitclerc, Canadian wheelchair racer and Senator

CHAPTER FOUR

From Flipping Mindset to Flipping Houses

ONE THING I APPRECIATE FROM MY TIME at the small independent office was learning from the owner. He was a serious real estate investor who owned multiple homes in town. He taught me how the investment game works, or as I remember it, he piqued my interest about passive rental income. I did not know then what I know now—that making money when you are not working is a key part of the formula for wealth.

I watched the owner of the office, as well as others in the real estate game. I learned that a person could carry up to ten mortgages on home purchases. That was a great option for someone like me who did not have a lot of cash to invest. I dove into the tools and rules for real estate investing to learn what I must do to make money while I still worked another job.

I had a good job in the state police, a secure job with a decent salary. I had good credit to leverage purchasing power to buy properties. I decided to go for it!

Since I didn't have a lot of cash to put down to purchase an investment property at the time, I applied a tactic we commonly used at the time. The technique was to inflate the sales price then use the equity after appraisal for closing costs, down payments, and repairs. This was powerful knowledge! It helped me get into the real estate investing game.

I purchased my first investment property while working at that small office. It was a house located at 5 Lawrence Court in Sicklerville, NJ. Even knowing the tricks of the trade that I was taught, I didn't have enough money. Therefore, I partnered with my Dad. Together, we purchased it for 30k, with the tenant in place. The mortgage amount with principal and interest was about $500 a month which included insurance and taxes. The tenant paid us $850 a month. You can do the math.

Another trick was to look for deals like FSBO (For Sale By Owner) properties.

> *One day, I saw a woman putting up an FSBO sign. I stopped to ask how much she wanted. She said, "60k."*
>
> *I said, "I'll take it." I gave her my real estate card and said I would be back with the down payment in an hour.*
>
> *I went to my dad, who agreed it was a good deal. We came up with the $3k to hold it. I returned to my desk at the office to draw up the contracts. Then I drove back to the home only to find that the lady was not answering the door. When I called her, she said, "I'm with your broker now, he said he can sell it*

for me for more."

I was confused because I did what my broker taught me to do. Later, when I asked him why he did that, he said he thought he could get her more money. He didn't have much else to say. I felt violated. I felt betrayed. I felt like he stole the real estate commission on the sale AND the income from me that I would have received after I flipped the home.

That was the day when I realized the reason the office was a small-town brokerage. I will always be grateful for the opportunity that those brokers gave me. The training was on-the-job. It was the best I could have had. I realized that day, however, that their company culture was not in alignment with where I wanted to go with business.

Even with occasional disappointments, this was a great time for people like me who had little money to play with. Today there are more checks and balances in place, but real estate investing done right still creates passive income streams without having a lot of capital invested. Once you have about ten houses, the right ten houses, even with mortgages you can have a nice monthly passive income stream.

The key is to leverage the first to buy the second. With money coming in from 5 Lawrence Ct., we purchased 41 Memphis Ct. That's when I began to feel like a landlord. I moved up the ladder by buying my third house, a duplex at 12 East Ave. This property was in Glassboro, a college town with Rowan University close by, so getting tenants was easy.

At the time I bought the third house in 2001, the real estate market was spiking up in a spiral that became one of the great real estate markets of our times. I call these houses my Big 3 because they truly started it all for my real estate investing career.

The Church House Flip

The first flip that convinced me to stop tying up my credit is a classic story. At that time no one wanted to buy or sell homes in Camden, NJ. I could not blame them. It was nine square miles of the most dangerous landscape in the US. Camden was ranked nationally with a high murder rate and a population living in poverty.

Of course, I was not concerned by this. I was a trooper. I did not look at risk in the way that most normal human beings would. Remember, I was this alpha male, wearing the blue and gold uniform. At the time most of us thought we were invincible. I sure did!

I was also the go-to realtor in Camden. No homeowner wanted to go into the City to find an agent. Most real estate agents wanted to avoid going into Camden. I was already in Camden as a trooper making it an easy choice for home owners and real estate agents to direct business my way.

> *A realtor from Remax asked me if I was interested in a property in Camden close to the Waterfront. It was a recently remodeled duplex. I looked at it then purchased it with 100% financing, which was running rampant at the time. After the purchase I went to the property to figure out my plan. As I walked out of the house, a well-dressed gentleman approached me.*
>
> *"Do you own this house?" he asked.*
>
> *"Yes, I do, sir."*
>
> *"How much are you selling it for?"*
>
> *I paused for 10 seconds that felt like 10 minutes. I was quickly running numbers in my mind. I concluded that if I could double my money, I would be okay with not making the passive income this duplex would bring me. With two renovated units, I stood to make nearly $1,000 every month, of passive income.*

> *Business is business, so I said to the gentlemen, "It's not really for sale but if I did put it on the market, it would have to be no less than 120k."*
>
> *"Sold!" says he. "I'm the pastor of the church next door. We need this house for my church."*

That opened doors for me as an investor. I finally had a substantial amount of my own cash to work with to pay for repairs, closing costs, and fees. I could avoid having mortgage payment piled on top of mortgage payment.

Expansion was a reasonable next step. I started to sell off the Big 3 to get into better neighborhoods. The goal was to have more equity and passive income between the mortgage and the amount I collected in rent.

I doubled my money on 12 East Ave. because Glassboro State College became Rowan University. All the buzz and new enrollments caused the values in Glassboro to jump up.

My overall strategy was to purchase a lot of homes and hold them. At one point I had nearly 40 units. I even started a property management company which I used to manage my real estate client's homes, too. (That property management thing was tough. More accurately, I had horrible, ineffective systems in place at that time.)

I sold my smaller investments, like 5 Lawrence and 41 Memphis Court, to buy larger investments like a shore house, land, and properties to flip. Later I even picked up commercial properties, like strip malls and office buildings.

I had a dream to own a shore house. At the time I started looking, Wildwood and Brigantine were the most affordable areas to buy into at the Southern NJ shore.

Brigantine was an exciting opportunity due to the Borgata Hotel and Casino that was under construction. The biggest draw was the tunnel which got you to the Marina district without going through downtown Atlantic City. A convenient access to Brigantine was an appealing option for shore goers, renters, and second homeowners. During my search for shore properties, I found a duplex in Brigantine.

At the same time, I found a six-unit complex in Wildwood, a community also on its way up. What happened next was an interesting lesson.

Managing properties in Wildwood became more complicated than I anticipated. I drove all over the place as a state trooper, simply part of the job. When I expanded my investments to regional instead of staying local, I experienced more windshield time as a real estate investor, too. At the same time, I was also a supportive husband.

Wildwood had six units and tenants to manage. The drive was an hour and a half one way. Wildwood became more than complicated. It was a challenge.

To complicate the investment picture further, the duplex in Brigantine I thought was structurally sound needed to be torn down. I had mortgaged that property, paying 215k for what turned out to be land.

As might be expected, I eventually got tired of driving to Wildwood and dealing with that 6-tenant property. I sold it. As it turned out, I sold it too soon.

This was an important intersection. I was entering into a different stage of real estate investing. Sadly, I did not stay on top of my investment. Had I paid closer attention, I would have realized that Wildwood passed a zoning change. That change would have put $150K more in my pocket—if I had waited nine more months. Under the new zoning, I could have made those units condos and sold them individually, as opposed to the single unit I purchased and sold. I cost myself easily $150-300K, depending on what improvements I made.

That deal haunted me for years. I still think about it from time to time. It's those lessons that truly make us better when we learn from them and do not ever let it happen again.

For the Brigantine investment, I took a gamble. A big one.

I tore down the Brigantine duplex to build a brand-new home from scratch. It became a 4,000 square foot one family home featuring four bedrooms and 3.5 bathrooms, one block from the beach. A dream home. Unquestionably, my dream home.

Where was the gamble? It came down to how mortgages work. I tore down a home I did not own, which at purchase was appraised at 215k. When I refinanced the home after I rebuilt it, the lender appraised the new construction at $905k. At the height of the boom, it was appraised again at $1 million.

It was a big gamble for a long-term reward. I still have that home today. My family and I enjoy our time there. We will continue to do so for years to come. Investment is not always about the short-term profit to be made on a property.

Life Lesson: Parallel Paths

Here's a truth I want you to embrace: if I could do it anyone can. I started with a small investment. I turned that into a million dollar plus net worth in less than five years. That is an incredible ROI in anyone's book. All I did was use every angle the world gave me to succeed.

I learned from books, gained understanding from others who were more experienced, paid attention to the lessons they taught, and leveraged every bit of knowledge that came into my reach. As important as all that learning is, the most important thing I did was to take action.

Are you allowing fear to keep you from taking action? Many do.

Are you complaining about a lack of capital to invest? Many claim they do not have enough money to invest. Are you using this as an excuse?

I had $3,000 in the bank when I used $2,500 to purchase my first investment property at 5 Lawrence Court. That was not extra money—I paid all my monthly bills out of that money, too.

It's worth repeating this... if I can do it, you can!

The lesson is to embrace parallel paths until you are ready for change. Learn all you can, work your plan, and above all, take action. Small steps become giant leaps with the right plan.

LET'S THINK ABOUT THIS...

1. For my realtor friends out there: Do you consider it fair that you make your clients wealthy while you are just earning 'extra money'? It's OK to make money for your clients. You provide a service and are paid for it. You must also practice what you preach. Take care of you and yours, too.

2. It's important to educate yourself. Enlist professionals. Find realtors who are successful in investing. Their proven track record can help you figure out how to get started.

3. If you want to wealth build, sometimes it's enough to provide the deal to a money person. (Don't ever say I don't have the money, if you find a great deal, you will find the money.) If it's not a good deal, maybe that's why no one is biting!

4. Does fear or lack of money stop you from investing? What are you waiting for? Develop an investing strategy now! Let's Go! What action can you take, or put a date on and plan to take, to get started now?

5. Keep asking for help until someone is willing to help you. Join our Facebook group! Get yourself into a community of like-minded people with access to resources to support you. Just ACT!!!

Maya Angelou is a famed American poet and author. From the age of three to seven she was raised by her grandmother, providing her with a period of calm and stability in what would be a traumatic childhood.

Grandma ran a general store. One thing that riled her was people complaining. They'd complain about the heat, the cold, and myriad issues Maya's grandmother thought trivial.

Often Maya's grandmother would wait until the complainer had left the store, then say to Maya, "Sister, did you hear what Brother So-and-So or Sister Much-to-Do complained about? Sister, there are people who went to sleep all over the world last night, poor and rich and white and black, and they will never wake again. Those dead folks would give anything for five minutes of this weather that person was grumbling about. So, you watch yourself about complaining, Sister.

What you're supposed to do when you don't like a thing is change it. If you can't change it, change the way you think about it. Don't complain."

Source:
Maya Angelou, Condensed Chicken Soup for the Soul.

"People do not decide their futures, they decide their habits and their habits decide their futures."

F.M. Alexander, Teacher and Founder of the Alexander Technique

CHAPTER FIVE

Bit by Bit, Inch by Inch

PEOPLE WERE NOTICING JOHN CLIDY the realtor. My investing strategies were growing. My real estate sales business was being noticed. People started asking me what I was doing, especially the state troopers I was around every day.

In 2003, I was selling 70 to 80 homes a year, while purchasing four to five homes for investment. I continued that process, increasing the amount I purchased every year. Before I knew it, I owned more than 40 units, all delivering a generous, passive return.

Some of that investment action involved flipping a few houses and holding a few. I was flipping five to seven homes a year on average. In addition, I partnered with numerous individuals to flip homes. Mostly, I did these partnerships to help them get started or to help them with the money—just like my dad helped me years ago!

Century 21

It was only natural that I would meet agents and brokers from larger companies, many of whom I came to respect. A casual meeting with an agent named Dee Woods, someone I knew to be a solidly respected real estate professional, turned into the opportunity for me to move on to the next level. I consider Dee a friend. Thank you, Dee, for introducing me to a better way for me at that time.

It was at the end of 2003 when Dee approached me about joining Century 21. Dee and I had done some co-ops (that's real estate jargon for working with another real estate office other than yours). Based on our co-ops, she knew I was a hard worker who delivered. I guess she saw the potential in me. I never did ask her why she approached me for C21!

It was the right timing. I had outgrown the independent real estate office. The next logical step for me was to join a larger firm, to surround myself with more like-minded, successful people to raise my game up. Dee worked at a Century 21 office in town.

I interviewed with the owners, who ran a family oriented real estate office. There were a lot of great agents housed there. The atmosphere was open. I decided to join their firm. Within a year the move proved to be the right one for me. For the first time in my experience, I was ranked among the top real estate sales reps in the local market.

Of course, I still worked for the state police, meaning I

couldn't be in the office all the time. I started building a team to help me out. I called it The Clidy Group. Since my dual career track put me at minus 40-50 hours a week, I was only in the office to meet clients for settlements, signing contracts with clients, or to make an important meeting. Every minute in my calendar was calculated, every conversation meaningful and deliberate. Luckily, I am not the type of person who wastes time. My wife always jokes with me that I get right to the point and once I'm done with the conversation, I check out, I'm done. She's right!

One highlight I recall as a realtor from those days is worth mentioning. When I started out with C21, the #1 agent; had been on top for years. The wall was filled with plaques in his name as a top performer.

The first time I made #1 agent, he was congratulatory. I recall saying to him, "If I make #1 every month for as long as he did, then I would feel like I deserved the congratulations." Receiving the award for one month did not feel right to me. I was starving for more, I wanted to see my name up there every month.

A few years later, my name was consistently on top. Soon, it was the new normal. My name was plastered all over the plaques, just as I predicted!

When I was considering leaving C21, I observed something about that once great agent, something that made my decision to leave C21 easier. What smacked me in the face was his situation. He was no longer the top agent. I was. Yet, he was still there. Still selling. What had happened to his business? Where was his legacy when I replaced him as top dog? What would happen to him in a few years when the selling stopped? This top agent didn't grow, or at least that's how I saw it.

After years in the business, at the top of the company, I did not want a young John Clidy to come along and top me. It was an epiphany moment. I decided that I would not end up like that.

I always question, "What happens if I get hit by a bus tomorrow? What happens to the business? Can it keep going after I'm gone? What will happen to my family? To the agents on my team? Will they still have a job? Can my family afford to survive without me?"

How do you measure up in this area? Ask yourself the questions I asked and more.

When you reach a goal, do you think like a business owner or a self-employed individual? It's worth learning how to ask the right questions, don't you think?

If you haven't already read the Rich Dad's Cashflow Quadrant: Guide to Financial Freedom, get it. It's a must read for every adult in America. Reading his book will give you a deeper understanding of what I'm talking about in this chapter, if you are looking for more insight.

Robert Kiyosaki names and talks about the Four quadrants: **E** (Employee), **S** (Self-Employed), **B** (Business Owner), and **I** (Investor). There is no right or wrong answer to be found in the quadrants. What's revealed is where you are now and where you want to be. Understanding that we are in each of the quadrants at different times in our lives can relieve the self-administered stress we layer on and allows for a profitable mind-shift, when you are ready for it.

It takes a Team

I started to get more business than I could handle. I found part-time help to take my real estate calls while I was out fighting crime. I still had to, at times, run around while on duty to pick up rent from tenants, get contracts signed by customers, collect my commission checks, or meet a customer. No matter what, I always did my job. Real estate worked around the state police job. For as long as I did it, being a trooper took top place in my dual career path.

Being a successful realtor had a surprising side effect among my peers in the state police. I came to understand that there was a double standard, in a sense. My side hustle made money. My peers did not accept it. It became obvious that a side hustle involving volunteering without making money was acceptable. Had I chosen to referee, coach, play sports, or do anything other than make money, it would have been acceptable to pursue the side hustle on company time.

I thought my police peers had a crazy point of view around volunteering and making money. I believe some of my crime-fighting colleagues resented the fact that my hobby made me money. Even to some who felt no resentment, my side hustle was not acceptable.

I was not becoming known as a top state trooper who was a runner up to the Trooper of the Year Award for the work I did on the Atlantic City Expressway. Nope. I was becoming known as the real estate guy. High ranking Troopers—Captains and Majors—would call me into their office. I would think I was in trouble or getting a promotion, but it would be to ask me a real estate question.

In the early days, this double standard felt weird because I truly wanted to succeed at both careers, I wanted to be promoted. I wanted to be recognized as a great trooper, acknowledged by my peers. I wanted to be top dog as a real estate pro as well. Yes, I wanted to have my cake and eat it too, who doesn't want that?

What's the old saying, if you can't beat them join them? Well, my success in my side hustle was noticed, good and bad. On the good side, many troopers chose to join my team or use me as their realtor. On the bad side, a perception existed that I did not care about my state police job, which was the furthest from the truth. When I was there, I did my job. I was proud to be there—well, until I wasn't. Eventually I reached a point of no return. Progress as a trooper became less important to me.

Real estate teams were not common in the early 2000s. Due to my other commitments, it made perfect sense for me to leverage out as much as I could. Common or not, a team was the easiest and best option for growth while following my dual career path. Besides, people were asking to join me because I was making money. They wanted to know how!

Here's a lesson I learned later from a KW Career Visioning course. The concept fits here and was an invaluable lesson for me to learn.

Value + Validity = Thrive.

Write it down and see where it fits into your experience.

If you have value and start to get validity from your success, then you begin to thrive. People come to you, asking to work with you, as opposed to you soliciting people to work for you.

Investor and Facilitator

By 2005, I had earned a reputation as an investor, facilitator, and top agent. I began to sponsor Investor Seminars, sometimes with as many as 200 attendees. Friends and officers came, as well as the public. I would share my success stories around purchasing, holding, and flipping investment properties. I always told the journey of the Big 3, proving anyone can do it. No experience necessary, just make more income than you are paying out in your mortgage, plus you have some tax write offs, which is not a bad thing at all.

At each event, we also highlighted other investors, mostly the successes of my fellow law enforcement family who joined me in business. My personal success was a microcosm of their successes. The investment partnerships I forged with numerous troopers in Camden made me the most successful Camden agent at one point in my career. I continued to purchase predominately in lower income areas. It was from this base that I began to make real money which led me to venture into other markets in South Jersey. I wished at times that I'd be transferred to other units just to be exposed to a new crop of buyers and sellers for investment properties.

All the while, I was focused on investment, I was also building a sales team. Every new trooper or cop I met became a possible realtor or customer in my mind. I built a team filled with troopers and cops who saw my success as something they wanted as well.

It all started back there in Camden. Those Camden Cops really understood the side hustle mentality. They truly leveraged their off-duty time for creating wealth. I used to joke about pulling into the Camden PD parking lot because it would be full of luxury cars. Well, I found out why: those guys worked so many darn side jobs!

I love helping my law enforcement family learn about investing and doing what I did as a realtor. Over 100 officers and troopers have joined me—by becoming an investor, realtor, or as a customer looking to buy or sell a home. Some became real estate agents. There have even been guys who, years ago mocked what I did, come to me later to ask for a job or decide to invest through me.

The Clidy Group

The Clidy Group was truly formed out of necessity. I was selling over 100 homes a year and I have not sold less than 100 homes annually since. (I've averaged about 150 annually over the past 10 years. Still to this day the Clidy Group continues to sell more than 100 homes a year.)

Like any business, when service to your client suffers because you are too busy, it's time to make a hire. That's what I did with the Clidy Group. I hired people who would take care of business while I worked at the state police.

Gary Keller says, "Imagine life is a game in which you are juggling five balls. The balls are called work, family, health, friends, and integrity. And you're keeping all of them in the air.

One day you finally come to understand that work is a rubber ball. If you drop it, it will bounce back. The other four balls—family, health, friends, and integrity—are made of glass. If you drop one of these, it will be irrevocably scuffed, nicked, perhaps even shattered."

To paraphrase Gary Keller, *when your business life is crazy and out of whack, you're missing a person in a position or a coach.* I was missing both at that time. This is especially true when the business ball being juggled is a dual career.

I had plenty of contacts, investors, a strong reputation, and the finances in place. The issue for me was handling the dual career; handling the volume of business coming in along with a forty plus hours a week career.

I needed to be able to follow through on deals without losing anything. I knew my idea would work if I had the right back-end support. I needed someone to follow up on leads, schedule appointments and help process paperwork. We needed to get to the settlement and be able walk away with a happy customer every time. Service was the key.

Initially, I had a former trooper's wife work for me. Then my fiancé (now my wife) worked with me for a while.

> *Andrea is an alpha lady. She could run circles around me. She left work after we married and she became pregnant with our first child. All I can say is, watch out world after she raises our four children. I've learned that in marriages, each spouse has an equal status.*

After Andrea, I hired close relatives. While my team was always successful, I needed to hire someone with experience, who was driven, self-motivated, and who had a strong work ethic. More importantly, I need someone full time.

I was asking for a lot, and my wish came true with Vic Mangeney. Bringing him on was one of the best hiring moves I've made. Vic took so much off my plate. He took on the 80% stuff, I did the 20% stuff. We operated on the Pareto Principles

(80/20 Principle), before I even knew what it was. Which simply means, 20% of what you do nets 80% of your results.

Building the Clidy Group was phenomenal. I loved the business building process. The tangible financial rewards were only part of the fun. With an admin doing the 80% activities, I was now able to focus on continuing to grow the business while Vic handled buyers, the phones, contracts, customer meetings, and managed the marketing. It was a big relief to know that someone was always in the office to answer the phones and manage the paperwork. I was able to focus on leads and customer acquisition. Without customers there is no business.

Our first real estate agent was an investor and client. The word was out. Quite a few clients became agents after seeing what I was doing. I guess I made it look easy. They came from all sorts of law enforcement organizations and agencies, including police officers and state troopers. We still have several officers and troopers in the group or office.

> *You may have noticed throughout the book that I differentiate between a police officer and state trooper. There's a deep-seated—usually good-natured—rivalry between the organizations. I love my law enforcement family members. We each are fans of our own agency affiliation. Everyone believes our organization is better than any other, just as do those serving in the different branches of the armed forces. In the end, it does not matter which is best—we all put our lives on the line. That's what really matters!*

I always said I wanted to run the group like IBM. Well, that was when IBM was cool. I now say that I want to run it like Apple. Building strong, favorable client relationships has always been the key, regardless of what business I emulate.

We were big on client appreciation and education. We took them to dinner, gave them tickets to sporting events, treated them like family. I say, "Happy customer, happy business." The group knows the importance of good client relationships. It's a major part of Clidy Group philosophy. Your database is simply your business.

I used the training and support to build a strong foundation for our group. As the organization grew, so did the results. Our efforts began to bear fruit publicly when I received my first real estate sales award. From that day on, the push was even greater. Every success fueled my thirst to build a bigger business

Managing a dual career path—both high-profile, high-octane careers—was a challenge. One can only drive full-out for so long! Work life balance is a must. All the success in the world does not matter if you do not feel good about what you're doing, who you are sharing the journey with, and the lives that you are changing along the way.

Earning My Education When Dual Career became Triple

Learning is valuable. Knowledge comes from living life. There are incredible resources available today to educate yourself. Education was not a big deal in my family. My parents were not tough on me about going to school or getting good grades. They were big on doing the best that I could.

I did not take my first go at college seriously. I was more interested in playing football than gaining useful knowledge.

I decided to go back to school for a do-over. I did take the second round seriously. I'm proud to say that in May 2004, I earned my master's degree in Human Resource Development from Seton Hall University. This was done while still working both careers. It was a bold move, but I had to do it. The decision was both personal and professional.

When I went back to receive my master's degree, I was more mature and accountable to myself. It sure helped that I had accumulated a tremendous amount of experience as a State Trooper and as a real estate professional. I was a totally different person than the guy who was in college to play football.

This time, I had measurable goals. The discipline to earn my post graduate degree was internal. I did it without anyone or anything pushing me.

I focused on human resource development for several reasons. First, I have a gift of getting along with people. Second, the gift also allows me to intuitively assess an individual's character and motives. Third, the responsibility of leadership I discovered in myself was serious to me.

The leadership roles I played in the State Police taught me that everyone depends on their leader for direction, support, expertise, and livelihood. In the case of the State Police, people depended on me to protect their lives.

Getting the master's degree gave me the credentials I felt I deserved. Pursuing the degree gave me the added satisfaction of earning what others could not give me—self-respect and a high level of self-esteem.

As Troopers, we learn preparation saves lives. As an entrepreneur, we learn success is preparation meeting opportunity. The entrepreneurial goal is to build a successful organization from the ground up. I needed to make sure I was well-equipped to lead this new organization successfully.

This desire for educational recognition was real. Real estate was the motivation. I could sense a higher aim in myself. I had a clarity of direction more solid than ever before.

I teach a lesson for business that I learned first as a trooper. We were taught to never be complacent. We were taught to always know where a driver's hands are when we approach on a car stop. As long as we could see their hands, we would not be hurt. No hands visible could mean this would be your last car stop because they could be holding a gun aimed at you.

In business, your complacency won't end your life, but it will kill your profits! I don't want you to die. Nor do I want to kill your profits. Do not be complacent!

Life Lesson: Change

The lesson from this chapter is to recognize when it's time to leave. Perhaps more accurately, use this lesson to evaluate your choice. Choose the right intersection when your new path is ready to step into. Be sure the path you are walking away from remains strong and viable without you there.

This chapter talks about creating a business and organization of which you are proud. Create your version of Apple.

Understand that you cannot create an incredible organization on your own. You must have incredible people inside your organization.

The key is to attract talent who will share your vision. A big part of that is ensuring you continue to learn and grow personally. How can we hire incredible people if we do not continue to grow?

What would your organization look like if it were to grow only to the level of personal and professional development where you are right now?

Are you ready to grow? Are you ready to act? I hope so! Complacency is a killer of profits and life.

NEVER BE COMPLACENT in business or life!

LET'S THINK ABOUT THIS...

1. For my dual career readers, just imagine that you are doing incredible work in both careers. In one career, you truly excel. What would your success look like if that career was your ONLY career? How long would it take for you to see differences in your rate of growth if you were focused on ONLY that one career? A few months? Years?

2. How important is having leverage? Everyone always thinks they need to do it all. That's not the case, you do not. Leverage is the key. You need to focus on the tasks you do best.

3. Take me as an example. I had to find someone to run my business while I was a state trooper. I hired someone better than I was at the part of the business I didn't want to do, didn't have time to do, and wouldn't excel in any way. Mastery is vital for success. I focused on my niche, which was investors. I created a quarter of a million dollar business which lead to a multimillion-dollar organization called the Clidy Group. Thanks to focusing on doing what I do best and leveraging the Big 3, I was able to change thousands of lives and my family's lives are better as a result.

4. I cannot repeat this enough: NEVER be complacent in life or business. Look carefully at your commitments. Are there areas where you are disconnected? Wishy-washy? Ambiguous? Make a commitment to remove complacency from your life.

For most of us, life would be difficult without motor vehicles. They have proved to be a convenience, and though a drain on the environment, provide countless necessary benefits to us in many ways.

This wasn't always the case. The first ever horseless carriage was built in 1769 by a Frenchman named Nicolas-Joseph Cugnot. It was an enormous three wheeled, steam powered, gun carriage, which traveled along at the break-neck speed of 1 kilometer per hour.

I can't imagine many people saw much benefit in Cugnot's horseless carriage, at the time. It was expensive, ultra-noisy, and it couldn't match the pace of even the oldest nag of a horse. Yet from that horseless carriage came a revolution.

Sometimes we need to remind ourselves that it's OK to start small, with an idea that seems crazy, then work to grow your concept from an embryonic vision into something great.

"First, they'll call you crazy, then they'll ask you how you did it."

~Unknown

CHAPTER SIX

Sustainability

SEPTEMBER 11, 2001. *The day that the world would change forever. The deadliest day of our American History, when we were attacked by terrorists.*

Law Enforcement is the kind of career you get paid for what you might have to do, not always what you do. 9/11 was one of those situations. I think every American can recall where they were when the attacks occurred.

I was at the Deerfield Municipal Court for a court appearance. When we heard the news, it was an eerie feeling shared among the entire courtroom. There was a moment of bonding between criminals, prosecutors, judicial staff, troopers, and other courtroom participants.

I knew I could get a call to duty at any moment, especially since at that moment, I was considered nonessential personnel. I was not on the road. I was at that time assigned to the Alcoholic Beverage Control Unit.

As expected, I got the call a few hours later from my supervisor. I was to report and get geared up. An assignment would be given out. I should be prepared to stay a few nights. I would be working 12-hour plus shifts with mandatory overtime.

One of the planes that was attacked left out of the Newark Airport. I later found out that hundreds of NY/NJ Port Authority officers were killed that day. A majority of the officers who work the Newark Airport detail and other major ports inside of NJ, like tunnels and bridges were lost. The NJ State Troopers stepped into action. We filled in for the slain officers, taking up positions to secure the Newark Airport, Caven Point, and all the tunnels and bridges.

During this time, we were unsure if the attacks would continue. I remember not sleeping for a few days. We were always on alert, especially while working the details. There were many questions and no answers. During those early hours and days after the attack we were uncertain about what was going to happen or when.

This was a time when I felt proud to be able to do something of value in support of the horrific event. It was a time when Americans honored what we do as police officers. I felt exceptionally proud to be a NJ State Trooper defending our state and our country.

When I was not assigned to the Newark Airport partnering with National Guard, I would have a patrol detail touring around the Caven Point, tunnels, and bridges. Can you imagine NYC on a Saturday night with not one car on the road other than my patrol car? That was one of the eeriest times I remember as an officer in my entire career.

I remember driving down to the tower site where they were looking for people, digging through the massive rubble, hoping against hope to pull out even one survivor.

It was quiet. No radio. No city sounds. Nothing. I thought about how lucky I was to be alive. I thought about how sad I felt for those who did not make it. And their mourning families.

That could have easily been me.

As a trooper, I always hoped to go home after my shift. And I did. Working as a first responder holds no guarantee of safety. So many first responders unfortunately did not make it home that day. I would like to take a moment to thank the brave men and women who did not make it out, and the ones who lived to tell about it. Thank you for everything you did.

I pray for the family members of the lost heroes and the victims of terrorism who went to work and did not come home at the end of the day. I continue to pray for you all.

FOR THE REST OF US, LIFE GOES ON. Our great country is changed forever. Through adversity comes triumph.

The only positive outcome of the 9/11 attacks might be the solidarity our country (and the world) felt, along with a renewed commitment to living life without fear.

Robert Kiyosaki, in his book *The Cash Flow Quadrant* which I referred to earlier in this book, talks about the four quadrants that define modern business:

Employee , Self-Employed , Business Owner, Investor

Ninety-five percent of realtors are Self-Employed. And like any self-practitioner, if you go on vacation or are sick, your business stops. When I understood the quadrant concept, I chose to move into the Business Owner and the Investor quadrants. This is a position where systems and processes run the business, not one single individual.

That was one of the biggest reasons I eventually chose to leave C21 for KW. Keller Williams at that time, was a strong training and coaching company with a powerful real estate platform. This move allowed me to learn how to think and act like a business owner, as opposed to a self-employed individual.

I saw first-hand how the world works for the self-employed. My dad was a self-employed roofer. He was smart. He worked hard. If he could not work or measure jobs to get more business or take care of his current customers in need, his company stopped when he stopped.

One time, when I was in college, he was on a job and jumped off a ladder. Unfortunately, his ring was attached to the ladder and his finger ripped off his hand. Luckily someone was quick-thinking enough to put his finger on ice. Some function was saved. Nonetheless, while he was out of commission, no money came in.

That had an impact on our entire family. I was still in college where I worked several jobs already because our family did not have the money to help me with expenses (nor did I want them to).

Those experiences stick with you for life. My dad taught me without even trying to. Working harder does not necessarily mean more money. Self-employed is not truly a business. I choose to make money when I am asleep.

Thanks, Dad, for instilling a work ethic in me because hard work, mixed with processes and systems, is a deadly combination for success!

Two things my wife says: I know how to hire and how to fire! I am hard to work for. I do know that. I demand the best in everyone. I will not let you off the hook. In the early days, I was known to throw projects at people and expect them to be done without clear instructions. In time, I learned the importance of leadership to success. I learned that when I provide clear expectations that require accountability and tracking, we get results.

I credit Gary Keller and Keller Williams for much of my training around leadership development. Starting with identifying the behavioral style of a leader or understanding how that style works within different roles, leadership changes on a daily basis. Expectations are set. Accountability must be assigned and managed. Leaders must lead by example and teach how to fish rather than do the fishing. Keller Williams training platform covers all bases.

How we show up as a leader is essential. What we do in the first 30, 60, and 90 days sets us up as leaders for the remainder of our leadership experience with that particular hire. How much confidence do you think there is in a leader who, on the first day of work, pops in a video and says, "Watch this and good luck working for me!", then walks away? Effective leaders set the tone on the first day and clearly explain the expectations, standards and most importantly, share the vision.

That is the kind of leadership that builds sustainable businesses.

Who You Hang With Matters

Jim Rohn, motivational speaker and self-help guru says, "You are the average of the five people you spend the most time with."

I believe there is truth in what he says. Your goal is to achieve better in life. When the people you are around do not share that goal, then you are at risk to adopt their poor habits. Successful people read to feed their minds. Leaders invest in themselves and their future. Do the kind of leaders you want to follow practice great family values and live faith-based lives? Then surround yourself with leaders and associates who embrace the same values.

It's like this. Let's say you are at the gym working out. You have a decent body and you're hot from the workout so you take off your shirt. Then your friend comes in. You put your shirt back on. His conditioning is not as good as yours. You feel embarrassed for him. The business people you hang out with are the same. Don't hang out with business associates who you are embarrassed for, or to be with. When everyone around you is in shape, it's no big deal!

We can each be a role model for adults, too. Lead by example at work and in life. Treat people how you want to be treated. Exhibit the traits and behaviors of a leader as a leader, whether at home or at work.

Treat all with respect. Who you hang with matters.

Dual Career

Many people say to me, how do you do it? How do you work two full time jobs? Little do they know, I have several jobs, or may I say passive income streams.

In any job, I think you get in there, figure out the process, then master it. Self-mastery is important no matter if you clean cars, sell homes, or work at the post office. Take pride and nail whatever you do. I was able to do the state police job and real estate both at a pretty high level. My challenge came when I was juggling too many things and ceased to excel. It became unacceptable to me that my work was taking a toll on my family life. The family part of the equation, to me, is the most important part.

Are you following a dual career track? Ask yourself these questions:

- What is the cost to do two jobs? Is it worth my irreplaceable time?
- Are you spending time on a job that makes little or no money and takes a lot of your time?

My wife had a successful career prior to working for me and choosing to be a stay at home mother for our four children. About seven years into full-time motherhood, she felt the urge to get back into the workforce. She decided to open a business. For a short time, this put her on her own dual career path. She ran our home at a high level while owning a healthy spray tan business with a partner. She spent a lot of time and mental energy on her business, as expected.

About two years into the business, I asked her, "If you had a great year, what could you make?"

We ran the numbers pre-tax and figured out what her best income might be. That was an eyeopener for her. The money alone might have been OK for a part-time gig, if her time commitment was equitable. When she factored in the time she gave to the business, measuring that against the impact it had on our family, she decided it was not worth it.

Investigate, evaluate, and be realistic about what you spend your time on. Measure the return you get for your effort in more than money. I think we confuse working hard or being busy for being productive and profitable!

Many people take on a second career in an effort to leave their current career. My estimate is that 50% of real estate agents are following a dual career path. I think that may be true for other industries like mortgage and insurance, too.

I've been asked if there is a math equation to follow to know if it's the right time to start a second job. My answer is always, not really. Your WHEN ties closely into your vision.

What are your 1-year, 3-year, 5-year, 10-year, 15-year and, 20-year life goals?

What do you want to do?

Where do you want to live?

Who do you want to be with?

How much do want to make?

How much do you want to donate?

How many people will work for you?

The list of questions goes on and on!

You want answers to these questions and more. The answers you give will provide a guide to follow and enable you to envision what you will be doing.

Let's say, like me, you are a state trooper with four kids. You want to travel three times a year. Your wife does not work. You want a 5,000 square foot dream house for your large family. You want a second home at the shore or in the mountains. All on a 120k salary. That's not going to happen!

What do you need to provide your goal scenario?

How long will it take?

Do you need a good part-time job? Or maybe even better, a second full-time job?

Can it happen after you retire?

Are you waiting to retire to your happily ever after and it never happens? How many friends or family members do you know who retire only to go work another job to make ends meet?

Countless people work all of their lives to live a fairy tale that never comes true!

> *My wife's father worked his whole life with dreams of an awesome retirement, only to pass away at the age of 57. He suffered a heart attack brought on by the stress of being unhappy at his job. This affected our whole family. He never walked Andrea or her sister down the aisle. He never met his four fantastic grandchildren. Perhaps the most poignant and sad realization is that he did not retire with his wife, my mother-in-law of 35 years.*

Don't let this story be yours!

Setting up scenarios like the above for yourself helps you focus on what you want. Once you know what you want, ask questions that will let you make realistic goals to get it.

Evaluate the kind of work and the effort needed, to get the return you need, to meet those goals. Maybe delivering pizza or Uber driving will not get the money needed to live a life by design. That becomes obvious when planning and vision are paramount to hit your goals.

Are you doing what you want to do?

Seventy-five percent of the workforce do not like what they are doing in terms of employment. I recently read a report that states only 19% of people are fully engaged in the work they do. That's millions of people who are NOT engaged. I am truly sad to think about the amount of people who are dissatisfied with their work.

Remember, no matter what you do, don't sacrifice your values or your family-time for your extra money or dual career. Put your plan in place and know what you are doing before you sink time and energy to another career or job.

Life Lesson: Accountability

Part of your unhappiness in life can stem from the job you are in or lack of money to support the life story you and your family want. Maybe you do not feel that you are where you should be at this point in your life.

Well, join the crowd. Millions of people feel like you do. Now is the time to stop feeling trapped in your own nightmare. Get out of this rut and grab life big.

Do exactly what you want to do because life is too short! Today starts the first day of your entire life! Today you have two careers. Tomorrow you have your career, the one you have been waiting for!

LET'S THINK ABOUT THIS...

1. What are the average salaries of the people you spend the most time with?

2. What are the average grades of the children your kids spend the most time with? If home schooled, are your kid's friends learning the same curriculum as yours?

3. How do you help develop your children as individuals? As members of a family?

4. What's important for your family? What values do you have?

5. How does your career affect the above?

6. Are you truly doing what you want to do in life?

7. Why are you working two jobs?

Fill in the blank:

I will leave my current job as ______________________

and pursue the career I've been waiting for by __________.

Note that we've repeated question seven as a one-page declaration at the end of the book. Rip it out! Hang it on the wall! Copy it and put it everywhere and anywhere you will see it. It's your affirmation, your freedom statement. You want to have it in your face all of the time.

The Frillfin Goby is an ugly little fish that lives in tropical and sub-tropical regions around the world. It's not pretty, nor is it impressive in size, nor is it any good to eat. It's a nondescript little fish swimming in rock pools.

It's also a remarkable creature.

When you're a fish living in a rock pool the biggest danger is birds who see you as a fine meal. The goby has developed a technique to escape. It can fling its tiny body from one rock pool into a nearby rock pool, and if necessary, to another, and on and on.

It's incredible that the goby jumps blind. It cannot see the rock pool into which it will leap!

Scientists have discovered that at high tide the goby swims around the rocky areas to make a mental map of the landscape, noting where the depressions are that will form rock pools. Then from memory, it then leaps from rock pool to rock pool. The goby has a pea size brain yet accomplishes this stunning feat.

The Frillfin Goby fills me with wonder and reminds us to look for the remarkable in others.

"Don't let small thinking cut your life down to size. Think big, aim high, act bold. And see just how big you can blow up your life."

~ *Gary Keller*

CHAPTER SEVEN

Atlantic City

THERE WERE OBVIOUS BENEFITS to being a State Trooper. I had a flexible work schedule, a steady paycheck, influence, and contacts. The real estate business was working for me, too. The two businesses worked hand in hand. I was living the Dual Career life at its finest, or at least I thought I was. Both careers exposed me to interesting people and unique opportunities. My businesses were growing intensely. I was looking to stretch even more.

Life was grand. To top it off, I was offered another detective position, working investigation, but I turned it down. I thought working in the Atlantic City Casino Unit would be a good move for me at that time. Undercover investigations had been my niche for a while. Continuing in that area, I wouldn't have access to the 'fringe benefits' that went along with being on the streets. Atlantic City seemed to have a lot to offer in that area. On the line meant being in the field where the action was going on. I wanted to position myself for the greatest benefits.

My investment portfolio had risen from assets of $300 in 1993 to over $2 million in 2004. I was a successful real estate agent and investor. In addition, I was young and single. Going to Atlantic City seemed like the ultimate move.

Atlantic City Casinos

Known as one of the most loved leisure spots, Atlantic City, NJ is an entertainment showplace and casino resort. Tens of thousands flock to the Atlantic City casinos for gaming and entertainment year-round. The casinos run 24 hours a day, seven day a week. The city's sandy beaches, boardwalk, and amusement piers have been a family favorite for generations.

There is a dark side to all this glamour that most of the entertainment seekers do not know and hopefully never see. Atlantic City media tend to downplay the criminal activity that takes place. There is a lot to hide.

Unlike Camden where we policed with the locals, the role of State Police in Atlantic City was specific to gaming issues. We were there on behalf of the New Jersey Casino Control Commission. Anything involving gambling was under the jurisdiction of the State Police. Everything else was left to the local Police Department.

The job in Atlantic City was pretty good. We had a lot of flexibility. We operated much like firemen in that we only went out when we got called. This left us with a great deal of down time on many shifts. Most of the jobs were easy, but redundant. They involved thefts, underage drinkers, gambling, and handling defiant trespassers.

There are a lot of homeless people in Atlantic City. For most, the lure of the casinos is irresistible. Unfortunately, many, being cold and hungry, would steal from the elderly patrons at the Casinos. Our job was to remove these defiant trespassers, unnoticed if possible. There were many repeat offenders. Chances were good that the call we took at 3 AM to remove a defiant trespasser would turn out to be the same person we had kicked out the night before.

> *I remember a time I was in my state trooper car transporting a trespasser to the Atlantic County jail. I was negotiating a deal while driving. In Atlantic City our cars did not have a cage. These convicts were seated in the back seat with cuffs on. The guy kept complaining that the cuffs were too tight. I loosened the cuffs. He still screamed and yelled. I kept negotiating, ignoring him as much as I could since there was nothing wrong, he was only shouting to be a nuisance.*
>
> *He eventually settled down and said to me before we left the car, "Man, when I get my stuff together, I'm going to use you as my realtor."*
>
> *I brushed his comment off at the time, but remember thinking, "I must have a gift. After all that screaming and yelling, he wants to use me as his realtor."*

Being a playground capital of the world, second only to Las Vegas, Atlantic City attracts every type of criminal you could imagine. I learned about casino surveillance, security, and—a less-known fact—the high rate of suicides that occur in Atlantic City.

Night life inside the casinos was nonstop. The patrons were bombarded with attractions designed to keep them engaged in the fantasy of the casino. Many have lost their reality, their fortunes, and their lives at these establishments.

For the Troopers, the assignment appeared to have a nice trade-off: They could enforce the law and enjoy the amenities, including hanging out at the restaurants while waiting to be called to duty. Sometimes we stretched it a bit by hanging out as if we were out for the night.

We don't always make good decisions

In 2007, I was recognized as the #8 realtor in the country for units sold for all of Century 21. One unforgettable experience was when I had a $100,000 plus day. It was my own version of a Perfect Storm. I flipped a house that netted me over 60k—PLUS I had 10 closings that netted me over 30k!

I had in my pocket 11 checks totaling over $100k.

We were at dinner with another squad and some guy asks, "Why do you do this real estate stuff? It's a waste of time. I work overtime and make good money. I don't have to worry about tenants or anything like that."

Unfortunately, instead of just saying nothing or agreeing with him, I had those checks burning a hole in my pocket. I had literally gone right to work from closing. I did something stupid. I ripped out the checks, saying, "Here, you think $100k is a waste of time?!"

That trooper passed the checks around for everyone to see. This set off a mindshift in many of my fellow officers that was not pleasant for me. I moved from being a well-respected trooper on a promising promotion path to being a showoff. Suddenly, the attitude I felt from my colleagues was, "Who the heck does he think he is?

From that point on, I was treated differently. Rumors swirled that I didn't care about anything but real estate. Jealousy is not a good emotion for anyone, not the person being jealous, or the person being resented.

I was not entirely prepared for Atlantic City. Once the

newness wore off, I began pulling back from the good times. Then unpredictably, there was another major change in events.

A woman contacted me for the second time. Our first contact was regarding real estate. The second contact was regarding a traffic ticket. She thought I could help. That led to a relationship. Before I knew, I was in love. With that, my eyes were opened to a whole new world. The appeal of family life easily outweighed spending time hanging with the boys in the casinos. Andrea Waters accepted my offer, and we became Mr. & Mrs. John Clidy on December 2, 2005.

Adding Husband to the List

Being a husband added a sweet dimension to my life. Real estate and investing were lucrative and enjoyable. As a husband, I discovered something wonderful about our marriage. Andrea really valued being together as a family. Her heart was set on living as a family should, together. She believed in dinner together every night. She believed in spending time with me as her husband. Her focus became complete dedication to our marriage and family. I began to learn how much she had given up for me, beyond leaving a successful career, to take care of us.

Precious Family

My work life was challenging. I had a lot going on in my family life as well. In 2006, we built our dream home and my daughter Milana was born. I was a new dad. Life changed once again, in ways that every parent understands.

Taking calls at the casinos was not something any of us really liked. We would get called frequently to deal with defiant trespassers.

There was one guy we all knew to be a mean, violent drunk. One night, not long after Milana was born, I remember a frightening incident with him. As I put him in the cell located inside the casino, he spit in my face. AIDS was rampant among this population and was a constant concern for all first responders. I remember wondering as I scrubbed my face with antiseptic soap, *Why, when I'm making more than a hundred thousand a year on the side, do I need this?*

I was a young dad with a wife and daughter to think about. That was the time I started my mental countdown to leave the NJSP.

Of course, it didn't happen overnight. I was doing exceptionally well in real estate and was known as the real estate guy not the trooper anymore. I should be clear here. The year was 2008. It was not the best time for me to leave the state police. In 2007, I was in negotiations to partner with my brokers at Century 21 when the market crashed. We took partnership off the table.

I was fortunate when the crash happened because I designed my business to have multiple streams of income. I dealt with many investors, so my business did not take a dive like most agent businesses.

My second daughter, Sienna was in my wife's belly. Andrea started to have a difficult pregnancy. Her doctor placed her on bed rest. This was before the family leave act was available. My supervisors thought my request for a leave to care for my family was a ploy to do more real estate work. I had no vacation time because I used my reserve time off when my first daughter Milana was born.

I took unpaid leave. At the time this was unheard of. They were angered by my audacity. They were surprised that I would challenge their denial of paid time-off. They were not able to believe that I could leave for more than thirty days and not be paid.

This act infuriated my superiors because they could not see that trading time for dollars was not why I remained a trooper. Perhaps jealousy also played a part in their anger and inability to understand my situation. It would be difficult for most troopers to take a month off without pay and suffer no hardship.

The situation when I returned grew to be intolerable. I requested a transfer to a unit in Trenton. With a quick stint in IAB, the Internal Affairs Branch, I ventured into my final department, Solid Hazardous Waste. This is where I ended my career with the New Jersey State Police.

CHAPTER EIGHT

The Retirement Conversation

WHEN I HAD ABOUT 10 YEARS ON THE JOB, I remember noticing the young recruits saying, "I got 23 years and 243 days until I retire."

I would say to them, "You just got here! You already want to leave?"

There was always a lot of negativity and complaining about the job. When guys planned to retire was a common conversation no matter how many years you had in. The environment was not family friendly, there were many divorces, caused I think more by the pressure of the job than any other reason.

There are similarities in choosing a career to choosing a spouse. Having a successful career is much like having a successful marriage. In a marriage you ask yourself, "Do I love this person?" In your career, you ask, "Do I love this job?"

Most of us spend more time working our job than we do with the person we chose as a life mate. Being in a dead-end job or simply one you dislike can cause depression, divorce, and in some cases, death!

Is it worth your health or your life to be in a dead-end job? We have all seen the stories about disgruntled employees who go back to their place of employment and do deplorable things, like shootings or kidnappings. Your career, your job, is an important life decision.

I read a study in Forbes magazine not long ago that shares an important message. It reported that, "Whether due to stress eating or lack of energy to exercise, or simply due to the strain and drain of the job, there is a strong correlation between weight-gain and work dissatisfaction." Simply put, stress at work causes depression and anxiety. (Forbes, March 3, 2016, Ashley Stahl, You're your Job? Here's What It's Costing You)

It really is important to choose the right job.

The stress of working a dual career did not lead to depression for me, but it certainly did lead to on the job dissatisfaction. I've never regretted my time as a state trooper. I wanted to do it. I truly know that the state police experience helped me in ways that I could not imagine. Working in a job where lives are at risk every single day allowed me to push myself to the limit and beyond.

None of us know what will be our last day on this earth. It takes a special kind of person to face their own mortality every day. I'm honored and humbled to say I was a New Jersey State

Trooper. I was as proud the day I hit my 17-year mark as I was on the day I graduated the academy and finally received my badge.

The last hurrah for me was a retirement dinner where I said farewell to a 17-year career. Thank you to my 117th classmates. I'm grateful and honored to have worked with all of you!

My daughter reminded me about a story that illustrates how I feel, to this day, about being in law enforcement.

> *In November 2015, just a little more than a year after I retired, I almost forgot that I was no longer a state trooper. I was driving on Route 168 in Runnemede NJ, when I saw a police officer had a car pulled over. I could see a guy outside of the car speaking with the officer.*
>
> *As troopers, we are trained to pull over and make sure that the officer is OK, whether we are on patrol or off duty.*
>
> *I was retired and not sure what to do. So, I slowed down my car and watched closely. The man was facing me and I was close enough to see that the guy had a look in his eyes, one I thought said he was about to run off. Well darn it, that's what happened. The guy took off and headed right behind the spot that I just passed. So, without even thinking that I have no gun or weapon, I did what any crazy retired cop would do, I followed and chased the bad guy.*
>
> *I pulled into a church parking lot and I saw the guy still running. However, I'm in my car, so he has no idea that I was after him. I got closer and jumped out of the car. I chased and I caught up to him quickly and tackled him to the ground. Within a few minutes, a uniformed police officer arrived. I told him that I was a retired trooper. He asked if I wanted to be on the police report. I said, "No thank you, good luck!" I was glad to help out and I was on my way. I guess once a cop always a cop.*

From C21 to KW

When I first got the urge to own a real estate company, I didn't understand the complexities involved, nor did I understand my own motivation. Now that I have owned a real estate sales business for several years, I get it. It boils down to this: when the light switches on and you are driven towards a bigger purpose, you go for it! Complex business processes and regulations aside, it comes down to passion, purpose, and personal commitment.

I never wanted to own a company just to have my name on the sign. I love to lead people, which explains the regional role, state police, and running a team. The more people I can touch, the more I'm in my passion zone!

I think most people go into business to be extremely profitable. When a goal is identified, when an opportunity is taken on, I think there should be a barrier of entry. That barrier should be a challenging one.

If you want to be a KW Operatingn Principal, there is a barrier of entry. If you want to open a business to be the best, to be #1, it's vital that there are challenges to overcome along the way. Your success will be sweeter. More importantly, you will feel stronger and better about yourself professionally when you've beaten down those barriers. I felt awesome becoming a KW Operating Principal.

The Beginning of My Leadership Journey

Hosting investment seminars built my client base. This is how I filled rooms with prospects, clients, and partners interested in joining me or investing with me. In 2007, I was the #8 agent for all C21 for units sold, 171. I was profitably flipping homes. I had income generating rentals. Things were great—on the surface.

On the inside I was losing it.

I've mentioned before that KW offers great educational opportunities. One of the systems KW teaches demonstrates where I truly was back in 2007. The system resembles Kiyosaki's Cashflow Quadrants a bit. What we've done in the KW world is to redefine the process to fit our unique business models. E to P (Entrepreneurial to Purposeful) describes six personal perspectives that enable breaking through barriers. I was heavily Entrepreneurial in 2007. I was making money with no systems or process in place to facilitate sustainability!

I was applying nothing more than grit and determination to succeed, just like my dad! With a wife and child (at that time our first-born, Milana Leigh Clidy), I realized that it was time to think smarter not harder. It was time to scratch that itch I had to own an office.

When I think back on where my life is today, this intersection stands out as the very beginning of a leadership journey. I approached my C21 brokers. I asked them about partnering with me. I had a yearning to lead others, and not just a few, as many people as my leadership lid would allow me to lead.

In 2007, my brokers did not want to do anything with the current office in terms of a partnership. They were willing to partner with me in another location. It seemed clear to me they were not interested in growth; it was a suggestion made more to appease me. At the time, I did not see this as a problem since I had confidence that they would come around when I proved the new partnership to be profitable.

Then the real estate market tanked. All bets were off. Doom and gloom spread across the industry. Eventually it landed at our office, the top C21 office in the state at that time. People had to get second jobs, staff members were fired, agents merged, and most new agents left the business. Not to minimize the disaster for many, the single silver lining about the shift in the market might be that it really cleaned out the hobbyist!

Life Lesson: Mindset

As we grow and change, as we experience life, our focus changes. What we thought was important suddenly is not important anymore. The lessons learned that I've shared in this short chapter are significant. They were profoundly life changing to me. I did not understand the true cost of maintaining a dual career until I had a family to consider.

My mindset, when I started out as a single guy making good money to invest in a second property, was that of a young man working hard. My big plan back then was to have fun and show off my success. Then I met Andrea. My life changed. My mindset shifted to that of a responsible person who chose to act and behave like a professional. I think prior to that I was a hard charging person who had great results, but not sustainable results. With a family came an understanding of how to take life seriously while enjoying it more. Perhaps more to the point, family brought me to understand that what I truly want out of life is to change more lives than just my own. The only way I knew how to do that was through real estate and leadership.

Your journey won't be exactly like mine. You may find your success in a completely different way. What will be the same, however, is your choice to adopt a mindset that enables you and opens the doors to the success you envision.

My journey as an investor, as a realtor with C21, as a team-builder would eventually lead me to KW, where I found like-minded people and a system to allow me to flourish with no ceiling to where I could take it!

Where will your journey take you? Whatever you choose, no matter if you love it or not, your experiences in this journey will make you a better person. Learn from your life lessons. Choose to mold your mindset and create a future wherever your journey takes you!

LET'S THINK ABOUT THIS...

1. As you shift your mindset, things that were important are not anymore. Change is a part of this journey. Priorities, goals, and desires change and grow as your mindset expands. Reflect on where you are today. What's different from six months ago? What do you see as possible now that six month ago, you would not have thought possible?

2. Jim Rohn says, "You are the average of the five people you spend the most time with". Choose individuals wisely. Do you hang with a crowd that supports your dream?

3. Is your job in alignment with your character and who you are? Expand your answer to explain why (or why not).

4. What can you do to change or improve on your answer to the previous question? What must you do to bring your job into alignment with your character and who you really are as a human being?

I want to give you a scenario. You're 22 years old. You do well at school. You land a plum job in a bank. You work hard in your new job. Life is looking good. One day your boss calls you into the office. He greets you with the words, "We are terminating your employment. Your work isn't good enough, you're too different and don't fit in."

That's what happened to young Brett Kelly. He lost his confidence in himself, lost all sense of purpose and direction. He slipped into a routine of getting up late and wasting the day watching daytime TV.

One day Brett noticed how passionate a talk show guest was about her job, the way she so obviously enjoyed what she was doing and gained energy from it. "That's what I want," he said to himself. "That type of energy and passion."

He figured people who were successful in their chosen career knew a secret, so he made up a list of prominent people he admired—and set out to interview them and discover their secrets. At the end, Brett was startled to find that the people he interviewed shared the ability to build high quality relationships. His book about this journey is called Collective Wisdom.

"Working hard for something we don't care about is stressful. Working hard for something we love is passion."

~ *Simon Sinek Motivational Speaker and Author*

Section 3

Leadership

CHAPTER NINE

The KW Story–2011

I DID NOT MOVE FORWARD IN 2007, and not in the years between 2007 and 2011. I did not even look seriously at any other franchise, including Keller Williams, in 2007. I was focused on being a C21 owner with my current brokers.

In 2011, when the market was coming back around, my brokers were not as eager to partner. That prompted me to explore other franchises. Among the franchises I considered, Long and Foster, Remax, C21, and KW consistently remained on my short list.

My goal was to find the model that would allow John Clidy, owner, to be unstoppable and able to recruit anyone, from the new agent to the most successful agent in the industry.

Steve Pestridge, who had recently joined KW was a former Remax REO agent. He spurred my interest in KW. Steve and I had a business relationship. It seemed like he always had great listings. We often had great conversations about family in between our business talk. He's someone I respect. When he asked if I would take a cup of coffee with his Team Leader, George Denney, I said yes.

George Denney came to my office at C21 to meet me. Yes, I invited him there. I don't remember anything he said about KW. I remember his passion and the words he used, like opportunities and unlimited potential for growth. Our initial conversation rolled into me researching KW and eventually meeting the Regional Director at the time, Mike McCarthy.

Mike did not have to sell me on the company. As with George, I remember the words opportunities and unlimited potential for growth. Plus, I recall the words Profit Share. I did not know then that KW Profit Share would eventually replace my state police pension.

> *I also recall Mike commenting about a #1 statue I had in my office. Yes, Mike was also invited right inside my office at C21. I had my own private wing because I managed a large sales team within the C21 brokerage.*
>
> *It's funny I talk about that now. Basically, I was running a brokerage inside a brokerage. Many teams do this, but it's not really the right way to operate a sales team. Agents would join my team because I had a more competitive commission split than a brokerage would give them. I added agents because I had too many leads to handle. I provided culture, mentoring, and value as the team leader. I created opportunities and growth.*
>
> *I was the top agent in that office for many years. I recruited talented agents there, some on my team, some not. But I*

> *wasn't the broker and could not negotiate the deal.*
>
> *The statue Mike noticed had been given to me by my wife. It was a hand with one finger up, designating #1. Mike commented that I could be # 1 in Washington Township, and he was right.*

As the process of investigating the KW opportunity continued, I flew to Austin with George Denney to attend a class called Franchise System Orientation (FSO). This is a prerequisite to owning a KW franchise. It gives a comprehensive outlook of the company from all perspectives. Most importantly, it gives potential owners an idea of what to expect as an owner, as an operator, as a leader, as an investor with and for KW.

Because I was a top C21 agent at the time, George got me a private meeting with then KW CEO, Mark Willis. I do remember being enamored with his office; it was a true CEO office. I spent an hour with Mark. He reviewed my AVA which was a leadership assessment. (We now have our own leadership assessment tool called the KPA, or Keller Personality Assessment.) Mark was intrigued with my success as a realtor, a trooper, and as a real estate investor.

Mark and George Denney put the icing on the cake for me. I got the same message from different perspectives: unlimited opportunities and growth potential. Each of the leaders inside of KW said the same thing to me repeatedly. Years later, I'm using the same process, often the same words, to bring in my own leaders. Very cool how it all works.

> *At this time, we had four children. Milana, Sienna, Natalia, and John Howard. Natalia and John Howard are twins, born in 2010. Even though I thought about it often, I was not mentally prepared to leave the state police. Leaving C21 to become an Operating Principal with KW was about to expand my dual career roles yet again. Trooper. Real Estate Agent. Investor. Team Leader. Father. Husband. Now, Owner.*

I clearly recall the day I told my C21 brokers I was leaving. They did not fight for me to stay as, maybe, I thought they would. I truly appreciate those guys and thank them both. They were a class act who ran an incredible company. I learned from them and respect what they built.

> *Now that I have been an owner operator of several offices, I understand that their model makes it difficult to keep top agents. In a traditional real estate model, you must show extreme value and culture to keep top people. Sometimes you must go way off model on your commission structure to keep them. The days of real estate agents paying a broker more than $150k a year are gone!*

When I gave my notice, we agreed that I would have 30 days to move my office out of the private wing. When the top agent for many years announces he is leaving, it's disruptive to say the least. I was at my other job as a trooper when Suzanne Layser and Kim Phillips, two of my agents, reached out to me to say, "The broker says you gotta leave now!"

I was not ready to leave. Many details had yet to be worked out. I was still in conversation to finalize which path I would take. We decided I would sign on with KW as a Mega Agent Office while I worked on hitting the benchmarks required to be an Operating Principal. I love the fact that with KW, you have to earn the right to be an Operating Principal, it's not just about paying for a franchise.

With Keller Williams, nobody gets a franchise because of money. I had to earn the right by recruiting 40 agents and 12 cappers. A capper is defined as an agent who transacts more than eight units annually. At least five of the 12 cappers had to be an Icon Agent, meaning a head turner or top agent; an office manager from another franchise. Usually when you hire the icons, they bring with them two or three cappers. At KW, they set you up for success; they want you to be profitable prior to getting an approved franchise.

I was lucky to find a 1,000 square foot retail space down the street from my old office. We moved my 12 years of accumulated stuff along with my entire team of six staff out of C21.

The Keller Williams Mega Agent office began with the staff from the Clidy Group: my longtime assistant Vic Mangeney and agents Suzanne Layser, Carla DiPlacido, Cindy Reimer, Kim Philips and Melanie Geraghty-Wells. We launched KW in Washington Township with no fanfare. We were truly *Keller Who?* at that time. There were no signs anywhere in Gloucester County. The Cherry Hill office was not well-known in our area. We set up shop in a township that knew nothing about us.

Many doubting people said we would not last, which at no time ever crossed my mind. I truly believed then in KW (still do today) and what it stands for. I knew if I followed the model, nothing would stop me.

Before I started KW in the area, I remember hearing rumblings that KW was coming to Washington Township. I later learned that George Denney and Mike McGavisk had Washington Township targeted. They intended to open KW there but had not found the right partner.

As the Regional Director, I now understand this process well: opening a KW franchise is about finding the Operating Principal (OP). Then that person is tasked to run the play. It truly matters who you recruit and hire. It is no easy feat to become a KW OP.

In most other franchises, no matter how great they are, even McDonald's will fail with a bad leader in place. I truly believe the reason that 98% of KW franchises are profitable is because they care who they get into business with, and they've built a system that sets up the entire team for success. The process starts with the right OP and flows into the rest of the team. I have experienced this in my own KW franchise.

My team deserves much credit here for our success. If I had to name one person at the beginning whose efforts are worthy of a shout-out, that would be Suzanne Layser. Suzanne ran my real estate team. She allowed me to focus on recruiting and building the core group needed to meet the standards to launch a KW franchise.

I truly think she is one of the reasons the company stands today. I want to recognize Suzanne, and say, "Thank you for all you did to allow me to grow this company at the beginning."

Suzanne came over as an agent, but the admin I had recently hired was not ready to take on an expanded role. She stayed with C21. We needed more than an admin, we needed to support a KW satellite office in Washington Township. My team stepped up in a big way, wearing multiple hats as needed. We formed a core group made up of the first team members who bought into KW and my vision.

Part of the KW mission statement, God, Family, then Business, played a role in my decision to come over. These principles, as I came to know, bleed throughout the Keller Williams organization.

With the help of George Denney and the KW Cherry Hill office, we immersed the team in the KW culture and learned highly effective Keller Williams systems. The KW Belief System is what came to drive the culture inside our office. I am grateful for people like Jay Ricci and Stephen Pestridge who helped get us Kellerized. Also to others, like Mike McGavisk, who was supportive on structure and the financial side, helping to set up processes and get the franchise application completed.

WI4C2TS

The Keller Williams Realty Belief System

Win-Win: or no deal

Intgrity: do the right thing

Customers: always come first

Committment: in all things

Creativity: ideas before results

Teamwork: together everyone achieves more

Trust: starts with honesty

Success: results through people

The Cherry Hill KW office had several agents who lived in our area and worked in Cherry Hill because there was no KW in Washington Township.

Cheryl Dare, Dan Mauz, and Mike Lentz came over, as well Bob Dick who became our initial Broker of Record.

Once we had stability and a plan being worked, I attended regular calls with Regional Director, Mike McCarthy, Paula Hoeft, a long time Regional Operations Manager, and Michele McBride who was at the time Regional Market Center Administrator. This leadership provided guidance. Being held accountable by them was an invaluable help to me as I put those five icons, 12 cappers, and 40 agents in place. They lent their support across innumerable other tasks to be done prior to actually running the market center.

> *At Keller Williams we have a lot of Kellerisms, acronyms and abbreviations for our job titles and common terms. I learned a lot of them at Franchise Systems Orientation. The rest came gradually as we ran our business the Keller Williams way.*

I truly thank everyone who stuck with us at the beginning of the journey. I believe in the quote mentioned previously: "You are the average of the five people you spend the most time with." Who you hire matters.

This was especially true for us in our business launch amid a field of nearly 20 competing real estate companies. We had to get in business with people who believed in and shared our company culture. To fail in this would have opened the door to a cancer that would destroy our new company.

Turning Vision into Reality

I was out of C21. I was still working as a Trooper while building a new future with KW. I painted my vision for people because that's almost all it was then. I had no real office. I barely knew what I was talking about. I sold people the vision I had been sold on: opportunity and unlimited growth. That I believed in completely. That was a vision I saw clearly.

I started calling everyone I knew. I called title reps,

marketing reps and agents. I started at the top. I contacted the top agent at every franchise in the area. I was successful in landing one of the other top agents from C21, the top agent at Prudential in Mullica Hill, and Washington Township. I closed on a small office merger as well. Within four to five months I had a functioning and effective team. We were ready, willing, and able to build and grow a KW Market Center.

I later found a partner in 25-year Prudential veteran broker, Tom Duffy who also was looking for an opportunity. I was able to paint my Keller Williams vision to move him away from opening the Remax office he was considering.

I also attracted Haley DeStefano to KW who later became an Operating Principal herself in Swedesboro. I remember taking Tom and Haley out to Austin for Franchise System Orientation (FSO) just like George Denney did with me. I set up a private dinner with then CEO Mark Willis for us. Haley joined first, then Tom officially joined in April.

Months after leaving C21, we moved from the temporary retail space to a large, 18,000 plus square foot building. At that time, we only occupied the top floor, about 6,000 plus square feet. Our company, along with title, insurance, and mortgage partners, now occupies the entire building.

We also hired key employees early on. Employee #1 was Janeen Seagreaves who still is with us today, and Matt Teter who was with us during the beginning. Matt did some great things with us.

I think Matt's story shows what our company is about. Matt Teter was a young attorney who decided not to practice law anymore. He worked at a clothing company. The way we came to know him was pretty cool.

> *My wife and I enjoy brunch at Four Seasons in Philly for Mother's Day every year. This particular Mother's Day, I spoke with fellow patron Robert Turner who was an incredible business owner himself. I was casually telling him about the*

(KW) company I just launched. I mentioned that I was looking for a talented individual to run my company, to take on the role of Team leader. I did the same thing George Denney and Mike McCarthy did with me. I focused my words on vision, opportunity, and unlimited growth potential to explain what a person would get working with me.

Shortly after, I got a call from Matt Teter who advised me that Robert Turner, his mentor, suggested that we talk about a job opportunity.

I went through the Recruit Select process with Matt, the same process Mike McCarthy did with me for the Operating Principal role. I remember Matt was smart, passionate, and eager to succeed.

Not long after, we hired Maria Galleli and Sheena Atkinson. We grew from 60 people to 200 fast, in less than two years. I guess the people who said we would close in a year would not be happy now that we are the largest, most productive office in town—in less than two years.

Our shiny new KW franchise took root in the heart of a competitive real estate community in Washington Township. There was a successful C21 office, four Remax offices, a Weichert and Berkshire Hathaway Home Services franchise, plus numerous independents doing well in town. Being #1 in this market was not going to be an easy task! However, as I know now, KW is #1 in most of its markets when the market center follows the model.

Life Lesson: Begin Your Take Action Plan

If you do not have your career figured out, the first step that anyone can take is to make a plan. Don't leave your job if you don't have money saved. This is especially true if you have a family. Be smart and tactical about your move.

This should not be a spur-of-the-moment decision. Pray on this. Ask questions. If you're in a committed relationship or married, share with your spouse.

Eventually, you will want to write down your plan then have a mentor or coach (someone you trust) look at it. Speak to your professional service providers, including an accountant, financial planner, and attorney.

This is a huge decision. Make sure you cross your t's and dot your i's before you jump in the water. Doing it right matters. Figure out how you can create a life by design, not by default.

LET'S THINK ABOUT THIS...

1. Do we ever stop growing as a person?

2. Do we know what the future holds? Should we know?

3. Does the vision I cast include my significant other? My mentor? My children? Consider who you want to include as you begin to develop your vision.

4. Is it important to create a legacy?

5. Will my plan change the legacy for my family? Will my children's children know my name?

6. Have you done your homework on the company or leader you are going to work with or partner with?

At the Olympic Games, in Mexico, 1968 the marathon was the final event. The Olympic stadium was packed. There was excitement as the leading athlete entered the stadium. The crowd erupted as he crossed the finish line. Way back in the field, eclipsed by the other runners was John Stephen Akhwari of Tanzania.

After 30 kilometers, his head throbbed, his muscles ached, and he fell to the ground with serious leg injuries. He refused to stop. With his knee bandaged, Akhwari hobbled on. An hour after the winner, he entered the stadium, circled the track at a painstakingly slow pace, and collapsed over the finish line.

It is one of the most heroic efforts of Olympic history.

Akhwari says simply, "My country did not send me to start the race. They sent me to finish."

"To be financially wealthy, you must have a purpose for your life.... without purpose, you'll never know when you have enough money, and you can never be financially wealthy."

~ Gary Keller

CHAPTER TEN

Leaders Take Action

THE SUCCESS WE WERE HAVING with KW and the commitment to all the other hats I wore, got me thinking seriously about work life balance. How long would I continue to be a State Trooper, Realtor, Investor, and Operating Principal? How long could I continue being so spread out professionally? Clearly my careers also had an impact on my jobs as Dad, Husband, Son, and Brother.

Our office was successfully launched. We were solidly on the way to a great future. Mike McCarthy, KW regional owner of the

Greater PA region, texted KW leaders that he was looking for a new leader to run the region. He announced that the current regional director was no longer in the role and he was looking for someone influential, driven, and determined who wanted an opportunity of a lifetime.

I showed the text to my wife who said, "Sounds great. Are you going to apply?"

"Yes," I replied. I was still the Dual Career Man.

Even though I knew in 2007 that I would leave the troopers, I had not yet worked up the courage to do so. This opportunity felt like taking a leap of faith and stepping off a high cliff without a bungee cord harness attached.

There was a huge gap in both time and education between making the decision to take that leap of faith and building the platform of belief that enabled action. In the end, it came down to me reaching the point where I had enough motivation to act AND had built enough financial safety for my family to make that act possible. After tons of discussion and prayer. It came down to recognizing that, regardless of what proverbial final straw pushed me into action, my wife and I agreed I had to go for it.

Leaving Six Figures

I finally spoke to my Lieutenant, a 28 year veteran who could have left the state police three years earlier.

"I'm leaving the state police," I said.

This baffled him. "Take the weekend and think about it," he said.

I assured him that I had prayed and thought since 2007 about it. Just to make him feel good, I said I would let him know on Monday.

What I didn't say was that my mind was made up. Finally, I had the courage to do it; to make the break, even if it meant leaving behind $7k plus a month of pension. That pension would be secure for the rest of my life in less than three years. I was walking away from it. Yes, forever!

Scary right? I thought so. For a lot of years, I thought so. But no! I finally understood that it was not scary. You see, I truly believed. I had done my homework. I had a solid plan.

You've been reading this book. I hope at this point you feel (or are beginning to feel) as if you, too can leave any situation if you are truly not happy. Opportunity is there for the taking to be happy. Do your homework. Make your plan. Step out into a future you believe in.

The opportunity to be in a regional area director role for KW afforded me the mental leverage to leave. Mentally, I was no longer a trooper. I was ready to move on. It felt good to tell my Lieutenant on Monday that I was done.

Then Monday came around. NJSP had no idea of what to do with me. In essence I resigned, even though to me it was a retirement. It's not normal to resign with a job like this, as I stated earlier. To my knowledge, I could not find even one person who had left three years shy of collecting a pension for life unless they had been killed, fired, or had hit the lottery!

A few days later, I met with the Captain. Whenever I'd met this Captain face-to-face previously, he was not usually courteous or nice to me. For some reason, that day when I stated my intention of retiring before my pension was vested, he was nice.

He said, "Right now, I'm not sure of how everything will work. It will take time to deal with the pension, your gun, all these details. It's not normal for someone to leave three years shy of a pension for life."

He sent me to meet with the pension board where I had to complete all kinds of documents. Everyone I spoke with was unsure about what to do since this never happened before.

Finally, the day came to turn in my gun and my gear.

I felt horrible. I'm not sure what I expected. I spent 17 years with this organization. It sure did not feel like I did that day. I felt like I was being told, "Hey let's hurry up. Let's get you out so I can go back to what I was doing when you walked in the door." The last thing I did was take a retirement picture, even though I was not allowed to officially retire at that time because they said I resigned.

There were no bands playing. There were no thanks being given. No handshakes or pats on the back for doing a great job, putting your life on the line for 17 years. I had been in fights, experienced the 9/11 tragedy, survived historic hurricanes, been shot at, and walked away from car accidents. I had experienced countless dangerous situations that could have ended up differently.

When it came to the last day, I'm not sure what I expected. This was a moment I'd thought about countless times. Certainly, I never imagined that the real-life experience, the climax of close to two decades of my life, would be treated as routine.

I handed in my stuff.

I signed a form.

My 17-year stint with the NJSP was over.

One of the guys dropped me off then took back my state police car. Only guys on the job understand how much we love having that state police car. Some guys would not even own a personal car (even though they were not supposed to use the company car for personal). I think giving up the car was harder for me than turning in my gun. I wanted to say, "Take anything, but not my state police car with its gas and insurance—and no monthly car payment!" Suddenly my free car was gone and dang it, that one hurt!

Just like that! Flashbacks of those 17 years from the academy to dangerous situations to friendships made, went through my head on the drive home that day. I thought the party was over!

But, it was just beginning!

Courage and Faith: A Test of Leadership

My wife recalls that message from Mike McCarthy about needing a new Regional Director differently than I do.

She says he sent a detailed email out, not a text about an opportunity. She remembers me saying to her, "Read this. Tell me what you think."

That's where the discussion began about our family, money, and quality of life. That's when I really started asking, "Do I love what I do?"

Here is an important learning lesson. Make sure you have questions answered before leaving your job. When I shared my retirement plans with others, most people thought I was crazy to leave the state police three years shy of vesting my pension. Their old school thinking was, "NO! You don't walk away from a guaranteed government paycheck like that."

Then there were the successful people who focused on the future, asking, "What do you truly want to do in life? Are you happy? Does what you do now give you unlimited potential and opportunities?"

For me, the answer was clear. I knew exactly how much I would make when I retired from the State Police. I chose to create my retirement, not let someone else to create it for me.

Mike McCarthy did send out an email for the job opening of the Regional Director. He advised me it was a national talent search. In KW, the Regional Director role is a big deal. Out of 180k associates, there are only 31 Regions in the United States and Canada and limited Director spots. The person in this position is chosen by the KW President (at the time that was John Davis) and the regional owners (at that time Rich and Mike McCarthy) who partnered with Keller Williams years ago to grow the region, back when Keller Williams was *Keller Who?*

I know I said earlier I was *Keller Who?*, but in the early days the whole company really was *Keller Who?* Thank you to all the Keller Williams leaders who paved the way for people like me!

I met Rich and Mike McCarthy several times as I went through the lengthy selection process. I respect the time and effort they put into choosing who they got into business with.

To put this into perspective, an Operating Principal, or a market center position, is focused on growing locally. This is regional. It requires a different level of leadership! Once identified as top candidates for recruitment we went through a series of interviews, including one with the KW President, John Davis, who later went on to be the CEO.

Mike said he started with 25 candidates. It came down to three candidates. We were all talented individuals. As Mike tells it, he and Rich decided that, because of the size of the region they could use two leaders. A Regional Director(RD) and an Area Director (AD). He asked all three of us, "Would you care if you were the RD or the AD?"

He chose the two of us who answered we didn't care which position we held, as long as the opportunity was right and included opportunities for growth.

Mike made a decision to place Jim as the RD and me as the AD. I believe he made the right decision. At the time Jim was better prepared for the role. I had less experience in KW. I was still managing a dual career and wearing multiple hats.

> *I believe that as I plugged into KW and became a student of leadership, I turned into an entirely different person for the better, one who wants to lead leaders. When I eventually became the RD, the role embossed who I am as a human being and allowed me to grow as a leader. That is the RD role: we lead the Operating Principals. These individuals are mostly millionaires and highly successful people themselves. In our region we have OP/Investors who are worth more than one hundred million dollars, and even one billionaire investor in our region. So, it is an understatement to say I need to be on my game every day.*

Life Lesson: Courage

Being Comfortable with the uncomfortable is what happens when you challenge yourself away from the status quo. You start to say that I'm no longer going to accept mediocrity. I will do exactly what I want to do in my life. No one will stop me. Do not let self-doubt creep inside of you!

Enlist help from people you trust, respect, and admire. Ask for advice while you are on this journey to truly do what you were destined to do.

One lesson I learned as a trooper is that you can never be complacent. Go for the gold, always. Start now. Do not let days, months, and years go by not doing what you are truly passionate about!

You are not alone! You are now a member of the Six Figures Community. Reach out to us at *www.leaving6figures.com* We are here to help you create a plan that will enable you to do what you want in your life. Do not let anyone derail you!

LET'S THINK ABOUT THIS...

1. Do you believe in yourself?

2. Why? Or Why not?

3. Close your eyes. Imagine your life being happy and doing exactly what you want to do. Describe what you are feeling. How does that feel?

4. Do you have a group of friends, family members, mentors, coaches, people you trust that you can ask their opinions?

5. Name them. Make a list and decide which people on the list you can go to for mentorship, for trusted advice, for coaching to achieve the goals you define.

I've never been one to spend a lot of time regretting what I did or did not do. Here's one of my favorite stories about how irrelevant regret is in the scheme of a full life.

A server told me this story one morning, about one of her regular customers, a really grumpy elderly man.

He had been eating in our diner every morning for the better part of five years. One day he left me $1,000 in cash for his $7 breakfast. Alongside the cash he left a small note that read,

'Thank you, Christine. I know I haven't been the brightest smile in your life. I know we've exchanged rude remarks a few times over the years, but your smile and hospitable service have sincerely given me something to look forward to every morning since my wife passed away. I wanted to say thank you. I'm moving eight hours down the road this afternoon to live with my son and his family. May the rest of your life be magical."

"It's better to look back on life and say, 'I can't believe I did that' than to look back and say, 'I wish I did that.'"

~ *Anonymous*

CHAPTER ELEVEN

Being Comfortable with Being Uncomfortable

LEADING LEADERS IS NOT EASY. It's necessary to always be on the top of your game. There are also serious requirements, including: travel, which I was not used to, leading events with hundreds to thousands of attendees, running weekly conference calls, providing one-on-one coaching to these high-level leaders, and many other tasks I had never done. I quickly had to become comfortable with being uncomfortable! For some strange reason I like that feeling, it keeps me on top of my game!

The crazy thing is, I had no real transition, no days off. I started the regional job Monday, May 1st, 2014, on the same day that I was no longer a NJ State Trooper.

Everything about the role as Area Director was new. I had many *firsts* in those early days.

Remember I was in a different world as a trooper. There, I worked with fellow troopers and criminals. Here, I had to evolve fast. I learned public speaking. I began reading with an eye toward learning and toward growing myself as a person. At the time, I was not confident about my knowledge being strong enough to lead people who had been with the company for years.

The role of Regional Director made me uncomfortable frequently. Taking on this role forced me to step up my game to a higher level. I had to reach and stay in a place that allowed me to lead leaders so that they in turn would lead their leaders.

My first regional meeting included myself and the RD, as well as our regional MCA, Michele McBride (who later would be promoted to AD and become my partner when I was promoted to RD). I was unprepared, even though the day before the meeting I had received a PowerPoint script. That first meeting I was nervous, ill-equipped, and embarrassed.

Right after, I signed myself up with Toastmasters, an international association for public speaking. I learned public speaking from just doing it. The KW Train the Presenter training taught me the skills. Being active in Toastmasters for a year enabled me to practice outside of the office and receive invaluable feedback from experienced speakers in a 'safe' environment.

I was committed to getting better at speaking. Take this lesson to heart, please. You must be able to speak in front of people to be a leader.

I can honestly say prior to taking the regional job, I read maybe three books a year. Now I read several books a month. I chose to transform as a person to become comfortable with the uncomfortable.

I recall attending the regional meeting in Austin Texas. It is a meeting attended by the who's who of Keller Williams. It took several months of self-talk to convince myself I belonged in that room.

I listened. I learned. I became the best note taker in the world because I was uncomfortable in search of becoming comfortable.

Every aspect of being Area Director, and later moving on to Regional Director, challenged me to be a better leader!

After about four years as Area Director, I was promoted to Regional Director. In this role, I help the OPs succeed on a high level. In some cases, I guide them to self-discover whether they are still the person for the job which is not an easy task. Telling someone who has been doing the job for 20-years that they are no longer the person to take it to the next level is beyond uncomfortable. I've learned that it's all about creating a relationship with these leaders so that they feel comfortable enough to listen to your advice, support, and coaching.

Everyone should have a mission statement. Mine is:

"To create incredible leaders in my world so that those incredible leaders can create incredible leaders in theirs."

I took the state police job because I got satisfaction and felt pride when helping others. I loved the power we had. I knew I would do good with it by helping, guiding, and being a good person in and out of uniform.

I feel with all my heart that I can help more people as a Regional Director. Getting comfortable with the uncomfortable allows me to influence the lives of nearly 10,000 associates and their families. My leadership could impact thousands of people.

I later became a MAPS coach, and an approved Keller Williams University speaker. Toastmasters was a walk in the park compared to the level of discomfort I went through to become certified as a KW University approved speaker. I did not make it the first time around. The roles I have accepted in this company continue to challenge me to be a better version of myself.

I speak internationally now, having recently taught in Canada, which was a cool experience. Being a Keller Williams University approved speaker allows me to touch lives far beyond those in my region.

I love the feedback that comes when I teach. For me, speaking and teaching involve truly sharing myself. I can touch many others while being authentic with my audience. As mentioned, I grew up humble. The only silver spoon in my background was plastic and painted silver. I believe people relate to where I come from and can see themselves in where I am going.

Today, I live a life by design. I have 27 passive income streams. I'm doing what I want to do. I no longer feel like I don't belong in that room with the *Who's Who* in Keller Williams.

I am creating leaders of the future who will do exactly what I'm doing. I am helping people change their lives for the better. It is gratifying to see leaders I have brought into this company changing lives as well.

Leadership Journey

R - Role
A - Alignment
G - Growth
E - Evolving
S - Summit

My soul R.A.G.E.S.

As a leader, I am at the summit of my leadership journey, bringing hundreds along with me as they in turn bring along hundreds more.

Now, don't think that I'm comfortable. I will always

stretch out for the next hurdle, because, as we are taught in law enforcement, complacency will kill you. In business it might not be a bullet, but complacency will kill your profits. The good thing about the KW leadership environment is that you usually are not allowed to stay comfortable, especially in a regional role. You will not last long if you are comfortable in that role.

Yes, I'm still uncomfortable. I challenge myself daily to be better. As often as not, these days I challenge myself to be a better husband, dad, son, friend, partner. That's the evolution that comes when you truly understand that being uncomfortable is how you stay alive in your soul, you become interested in what matters instead of the status quo.

Life Lesson: Comfort Zone

When I looked at the definition of comfortable, it states: *Physically released and free from constraint. Free from stress or fear. As large as is needed or wanted. Free from financial worry; having an adequate standard of living.*

As a leader, I don't like that definition. I do not want to be free from constraint or stress or fear. Being a leader is not easy. Leaders must grow themselves. Leaders must encourage growth in the people who entrust us to lead them.

Being comfortable is like asking to be complacent.

Let's not be comfortable staying in a job that we are not happy in, let's challenge the status quo.

Let's choose to enter the uncomfortable-zone.

Let's refuse to let fear or uncertainty stop us from doing what we are passionate about!

LET'S THINK ABOUT THIS...

1. Do you like to be comfortable all the time? Well, get over it, growth happens on the other side of comfort! Look at where you are complacently drifting along. Where can you enter the uncomfortable-zone? What steps will you take that will move you closer to your goals?

2. Do you believe in what you are doing? Are you proud of what you do? If not, what steps can you take to change this?

3. Do you ever challenge status quo or are you living a status quo life?

4. What changes need to occur for you to go after what you want in life?

Once there were two warring tribes, one lived in the lowlands and the other high in the mountains. The mountain people invaded the lowlanders and kidnapped a baby.

The lowlanders didn't know how to climb or any of the trails used by the mountain people. They didn't know where to find the kidnappers or how to track them in the steep terrain. Even so, they sent out their best party of fighting men to bring the baby home.

The men after days of effort, had climbed only several hundred feet. Feeling hopeless and helpless, the lowlander men prepared to return to their village below.

As they made their descent, they saw the baby's mother walking toward them, coming down the mountain that they hadn't been able to climb. She had the baby strapped to her back!

They asked, "How did you climb this mountain that defeated us?"

She shrugged her shoulders and said, "It wasn't your baby."

"You can't wait until you have all the answers before you act."

~ *Yvon Chouinard, Environmentalist, Billionaire*

CHAPTER TWELVE

What's Different in Five Years?

VISION IS THE NUMBER ONE JOB for an Operating Principal. I believe this to be universal for any leader; we are the holders of the vision. It is our duty to cast this vision for the territory or organization for which we are responsible. It is through the shared vision and commitment to the vision that growth occurs.

One tool I use to help my people draw their own picture of

our vision is available through the KW career visioning process. I often use a motivational story technique. It begins by asking this question:

> *Close your eyes. Imagine you and I sitting here five years from now. Everything in between has been awesome, What will you be doing?*

The answer will never be the same between any two people. Everyone has numerous priorities in life, including job, money, family, faith, and community. If the focus is on the job, then limit your answer to seeing a business vision.

For example, here's how I might apply this technique. Let's say an Operating Principal is launching a new market center. The OP states he will have 100 agents in five years. I know the average size of an office in KW is 200 agents. I know they do not have a big vision. If the OP says 500 agents, $1 Million in owner profit, over 100 capping associates, and gets specific, then I know they are thinking big.

Having a vision and being open to making that vision real is what allows me to exploit unlimited opportunity. My vision is that all these OPs and incredible leaders can fit inside my world, especially in terms of being an Regional Director. I do see my vision growing. Perhaps it will expand to other areas in life, such as wealth and legacy building. We must continue to grow.

> ***"Good business leaders create a vision, articulate the vision, passionately own the vision, and relentlessly drive it to completion."* ~Jack Welch**

To grow, you must think about the people who work for and with you. Be certain their vision aligns with yours. They might not see themselves in your world. When they are in your world, it may be up to you to guide them to the vision and help them embrace it.

Continue to state your vision to your team, sometimes every day. Jack Welch, former CEO of General Motors, also said,

> *"Leaders make sure people not only see the vision, but they also live and breathe it. Good leaders cast the vision of the future and motivate people to buy into it. They constantly talk about their vision and reinforce it with rewards, which may be in form of a salary, bonus, or significant recognition of some sort. Even without rewards, just sharing your vision as a leader can itself bring about the motivation your team needs to accomplish the most difficult of assignments."*

Life Lesson: Vision

What is a leader's responsibility? I would say to create a big, 'dawgone' vision; one that is so big everyone inside that organization can see themselves growing.

Think about what Gary Keller has created with Keller Williams. Think of all the people inside the Keller Williams organization, the leaders and the agents. Gary has changed the real estate game. He has given much back to the community and the industry. His vision helps Keller Williams agents and beyond; it helps the entire real estate industry.

That is leadership at its highest level. Do you have leadership in your world that makes you know and believe that we can all be better and think better? Sharing the vision is what leadership is all about.

Is your vision large enough? Are you a leader who shares a big vision that others want to follow?

LET'S THINK ABOUT THIS...

1. Is being a leader part of your plan for success? Why (or why not)?

2. How important is it as a leader to share your vision? Do you know your vision? If so, state your vision for success here. (Don't worry if you aren't sure, we'll work on it together!)

3. As a leader, should your vision include what your people want? Are your people in alignment with your vision?

4. What motivates you? What story from your life can you share that is motivational for others? Or is there someone else's story that resonates with you and supports your vision, your mission? Sharing your motivation story draws in followers and ignites your vision each time you tell it.

The Kalahari bushmen were made famous in the movie The Gods Must be Crazy. Their recent history is sad, for in the last 100 years the bushmen culture has been disappearing along with their lands. Many have grown dependent on government pensions and alcohol as an analgesic against their dislocation and loss. The problem is they've lost their stories.

"A lot of our culture," the leaders say, "is lost in our lives—the old stories are gone. Now we have nothing to pass on."

We can learn from this sad tale. It is the stories we pass on that shape and define us, that show us the way forward. In our stories we find meaning, direction, and values.

Be extraordinary and pass it on.

"By failing to prepare, you are preparing to fail."

~ Benjamin Franklin

CHAPTER THIRTEEN

What's Stopping You?

I KNOW WHAT WAS STOPPING ME: fear, money, uncertainty, caring about what people think. It was a solid mixture of emotions. I had to break each concern down to see if it was a true worry or if I could release it and move on.

We are complex beings and it's rarely one thing that keeps us in the same place. Change is harder than staying stuck. Fear, our beliefs about money, and the simple fact that it's easier to do nothing than face the uncertainty of success are the realities that keep us from our goals.

Fear

Fear: (n.) An unpleasant emotion caused by the belief that someone or something is dangerous, likely to cause pain, or a threat

When I broke it down, my fear was about the unknown. Who will I be when I'm not Trooper Clidy? What will happen to my family if I give up my pension? How will I be looked at by my peers, my family? The truth is that I have to be happy and do what's best for me and my family. I think me being happy is important, because if I'm not, it will affect my entire family

Another part of this involved what everyone would think. It was uncomfortable telling the state police I was leaving. No one leaves these jobs. Was I crazy? Why would I want to leave? Am I normal? What will my family think? My kids? Just bottom-line, am I making the right decision? Am I being selfish? All these thoughts ran in my head for years.

It comes back to mindset. I had to do what was best for me. If I was not happy, how could I make my family happy? My mindset had to shift to allow an informed, common sense decision, based on what's best for me, my family, and what's sustainable.

After giving my Fear Factor a deep review, I have come to realize that it wasn't fear of the challenge or that I might fail, or even that I might succeed. None of that stopped me, not truly. It was about uncertainty and the unknown. It was all in my mind.

Money

Money (n.) a current medium of exchange in the form of coins and banknotes; coins and banknotes collectively.

When it came to money, things were ok but not great. When you have four kids, you can never make enough money! My wife does not work outside the home. We chose for her to stay home and raise our children. It is my job to provide for my family so they can have everything I have and much more.

I look at it this way. There are no guarantees. Not with what we have or what we want. A new start up business may or may not be in your future. If it is, solicit help from attorneys, accountants, trusted advisors, and successful friends before you launch.

You can download a spreadsheet from our website at *www.leaving6figures.com* to track and see what your expenses and income might look like. We've also given you a snapshot of the spreadsheet at the back of the book. Check it out. We hope it will be as useful to you as it was to Andrea and I.

Regardless of your plans, please, please, please make an honest assessment of your money situation, what it is, what you want. Make sure you don't lead a life in which you never get ahead.

I read a book that I found invaluable. *Profit First: Transform Your Business from a Cash-Eating Monster to a Money-Making Machine,* written by Mike Michalowicz. It is a game changer. One statement, among many made by the author, especially hit me,

"Entrepreneurs, often by necessity, have to put on an air of success. After all, their clients probably don't want to engage with a vendor that's surviving paycheck to paycheck, but research has found that 83% of small businesses are. Small businesses defined by the SBA are companies that do $25 million in revenue or less." **~Mike Michalowicz**

The 83% the author refers to includes realtor businesses. A key takeaway for me is answering this question, "If I take profit first, could I pay my expenses?"

My answer is always, "If not, things must change."

So, after years of not truly understanding money like I should, I decided to hire a team to protect the money I make.

I hired a new accountant, as well as a financial planner. The team looked at my money, where I am, and more importantly, where I want to go. How much do I need for my four kids to go to college? How much do I need if, God forbid, something happened to me, for my wife and kids to live comfortably?

They dissected my current situation and told me where I am now and where I need to be. I love that they showed me and made my wife part of the process. Now we both know what our family organization looks like. My wife and I have monthly meetings to keep on top of our net worth. I love being financially literate after years of being financially illiterate.

Uncertainty:

Uncertain (adj.) Not known or established; questionable. Not determined; undecided. Not having sure knowledge.

Nobody likes the unknown. Will I be successful? Will I regret this decision? Will I...? You can fill in the *Will I* that best describes your goals and life choices.

I put 17 hard years in as a state trooper, not including the process to obtain the job, or the academy time. It was not easy to get a job like a State Trooper. 10,000 people started the process in 1995 and only about 300 troopers were hired over the next two years. The uncertainty around making the decision to leave three years shy of collecting a $70k annual pension for the rest of my life was indescribable. To call it a hard decision is an understatement.

I questioned how I could even ask if I should leave. Can I leave? Should I leave? How do I leave? Uncertainty was constantly on my mind!

Scary? Yes. Uncertainty was the biggest hurdle I had to overcome.

I asked everyone I knew whose opinion counted for me, "Would you leave a job if you knew in three years you would get

$70 annually for the rest of your life?"

I didn't keep any statistics, it wasn't that formal. I simply asked anyone who I felt would answer me honestly. I asked more than 50 people who I respected to get their opinion.

Even though it was informal and done over time, I kept track of what they said, of course. The compiled results were astonishing. A staggering 90% said don't leave, hang in there. Then I looked closer at who I asked and who answered what. An odd fact became clear: successful people understood. They really focused on my reasons and the plan I had in place.

I concluded that most, like me, knew what I had was secure and reasonably safe. They thought I should just hang in there.

The smaller group made up of those closes to me, such as my parents and wife, believed in me. They knew I don't just do things; I really review my decisions and put everything behind being successful.

Please don't let fear, money, uncertainty or any other obstacle that can be overcome stop you. Make your plan and go for it!

Let me be your inspiration, if I can do it, anyone can!

Life Lesson: Action Plan

If you plan, you can do anything you want. Don't leave your job without a plan. Fear, concern about money, uncertainty about making a change, all that and more creeps in when we think about leaving or changing jobs. You picked up this book for a reason. It is apparent that eventually you will take action to change your situation. You are not alone.

What's stopping you? The focus of this chapter has been on the obstacles that challenge us and keep us in jobs we don't want. This is where you lean on others who have done it before you. They said the four-minute mile was impossible—until Roger Bannister did it. Since then, the four-minute barrier has been broken by more than 1,400 male athletes and is now considered the standard for professional middle-distance runners.

When I left the state police three years shy of vesting my pension, it was unheard of. Not long after, others left the job choosing to forego their pension. Many reached out to me to say that I was their inspiration; that they were not happy but did not think it made sense to leave until they heard my story. These stories from my fellow officers inspire me. I love that people are going after what they truly want in life.

Never let anything stop you from pursuing your dreams.

LET'S THINK ABOUT THIS...

1. What's your biggest concern leaving your job?

2. Do you have the right team in your life to help make the right decision? (Accountants, mentors, attorneys, successful people we trust)

3. Can you provide for yourself and/or family when you make this move?

4. Do you have a budget in place? Do you personally know how much you spend and how much you make currently? You must know what you currently have before you can consider what it takes to replace it.

5. How much money will you need to make to survive? For how long can you make it financially if you don't replace your income immediately? Define the money you will need to leave. What's stopping you aside from the money questions?

6. Are there additional fears you have around leaving your job? Define any additional fears you have with leaving your job.

7. Is your plan in writing and have you shared your plan with anyone to get helpful feedback?

8. What could stop you from taking action to implement your plan?

9. Do you have a Plan B, C, and possibly D if needed?

Imagine you had a bank account that deposited $86,400 each morning. The account carries over no balance from day to day, allows you to keep no cash balance, and every evening removes whatever part of the amount you had failed to use during the day.

What would you do? Draw out every dollar each day! Of course.

We all have such a bank. Its name is Time. Every morning, it credits you with 86,400 seconds. Every night it writes off, as lost, whatever time you have failed to use wisely.

There is never any borrowing time. You can't take a loan out on your time or against someone else's. The time you have is the time you have. That is that.

Time management is yours to decide how you spend the time. Your money works the same; you decide how to spend money.

Don't be satisfied with the success stories of others. Write your own! Unfold your tale and bring it to life. You have everything you need to become what you can become.

"The biggest risk is not taking any risk."

~ Mark Zuckerberg, Founder Facebook

CHAPTER FOURTEEN

What's Next?

WHEN I THINK ABOUT WHAT'S NEXT FOR ME, what comes to mind is touching many more lives. I am now doing what I want to do in my life, especially now that you are reading this book. I am in a place now from which I can launch this book into millions of hands.

No person should be in a job where they feel trapped. This is America where millions of individuals come to create a new life. Often, they have limited education, no family, and no connections here to give them a boost up. Yet despite this they are able to become millionaires. If people with nothing can do so much, there is no doubt you can do whatever you want to do, whenever you want to do it.

It takes a vision, a plan, and the ability to act. Discover your vision. Create your plan. Go get your future!

Personally, I can go around the country and inspire others. I can help you with your plan to do exactly what you want to do. My plan says that I must touch more lives than I ever did. I must give back to more charities, I must get to church more often. I must be more present with my family and friends.

I've learned much over the past year, with Gary Keller as a mentor, about how to motivate high-level individuals. What I have learned is nothing unique: You build relationships and you continually add value.

"People do not care how much you know until they know how much you care." ~ Theodore Roosevelt.

The way to inspire more people is to care about them. Then it's a lot easier to lead them. For me, as I lead more people, I have to figure out how to give value to a larger audience of people.

I'm going to up my game as a leader and as the author of this book. I cannot help anyone unless I continue to grow. I'm totally up for the challenge!

I'm hoping each of you are up for your own personal challenge to nail your personal goals. I'm writing this book for two main reasons.

1. I feel a strong need to make sure no one ever feels stuck in a job.
2. One day my grandkids, and their kids will read grandpop's books. It's important to create a legacy.

I'll never forget what I took away from a KW family event I went to a few years ago (we call it Fambundance). Mike McCarthy asked us all if we could name the parents of our Grandparents. I could not. It was a pivotal moment. It was a scary thought for me that my grandkid's children might not even know my name!

I am creating a legacy where every generation will remember who I am.

What's in it for me? I will increase the number of lives that I help. It may be on a wider scale. That is why this book is so important to me, because it touches the people I cannot personally touch.

If this book inspires you, please do not stop there. Share it and tell others. When friends claim to be unhappy with their life, say to them, "No more! Do not settle for being unhappy. We are in a country where a homeless person can become a CEO."

You can achieve anything you want in life if you truly believe! Let this book inspire you today to do something great.

Life Lesson: Future

What's next? It is all about the future. What will you do?

Will you take the chance and not settle anymore? Will you allow yourself to continue growing as a person? As a business owner, employee, parent? In every part of your life?

The future starts today! Change the trajectory of your life. Now!

LET'S THINK ABOUT THIS...

Beginning on the next page you will find the **Leaving 6 Figures Take Action Plan**

Even if you did none of the other exercises in this book, this one could be a game changer for you. Each of the Life Lessons relates to the questions and actions in this plan. Go for it!

Reach out to us on social media—we love success stories, especially from our readers. Find us at *www.leaving6figures.com*

Leaving 6 Figures Take Action Plan

WHY do you want to leave your job?

Clearly define this. Refer back to the answers you gave in the Life Lessons sections throughout the book. Then write a definitive statement that resonates with you. Share your statement with the people in your life who are impacted by this decision.

Leaving 6 Figures Take Action Plan

MONEY

How much money do you need to leave? Is it in your savings already? If not, how much do you currently have and when will you have the full amount available? Are you in the financial position to leave now?

VISION AND PLAN

Do you know what you want to do? Is your goal to make a lot of money? Maybe both? Have you chosen a direction? Do you know what happiness means to you? What does wealth look like to you? You must place answers to these questions solidly in your mindset. You must be able to SEE what success means to you. You cannot share a vision you do not have. Define your vision and your plan here.

TEST YOUR VISION AND PLAN

Enlist help of people you trust to review your plan. Opinions from trusted sources are important but remember in the end you have to believe in it, even if others do not. Enlist their help to identify issues to overcome and revise your plan if their advice is valid. Be certain that this is truly what you want and that it is achievable. Do not act on emotion alone. This is your life and the lives of your family. Go back to the Life Lessons and list your trusted advisors here. Identify who you will share your vision and plan with. Set a date for when you will do this.

TAKE ACTION

It's time to make it happen. Go for it! Don't let anything stop you! Make your life by design.

REVIEW

Mark your calendar to review your plan in one month. Review again in three months, at six months, then at one year. How did you do? Did you stick to your plan? Are you ready now to take the next step? There will always be a next step. Remember, never get complacent or comfortable.

Leaving 6 Figures Take Action Plan

FUTURE

Make this plan about your legacy. Fill in what you can here and each time you evaluate your *Take Action Plan,* review this step and change it up! What will you be remembered for in 50 years? 100 years? 200 years from now? It is profound and scary, contemplating a legacy reaching far into the future. What will you accomplish for yourself? For others? For your family?

Gratitude and Thanks

Many of my police colleagues have done incredible things in real estate. They have earned more now than they ever could earn as a cop or trooper. A few earn five times more annually.

Bernard Woods, Rob Cecchini, Dan Torres, and Vince Parenti come immediately to mind. I couldn't name them all, but you know who you are. I love and appreciate all those who trusted me and chose to follow me on this incredible journey. I'm proud to say that I was part of their success in some way. This thought truly makes me smile as I'm writing it.

There are too many success stories to tell of people who have created significant passive income streams for themselves and their families. I do want to mention a few of my long-time investors who trusted a dual career state trooper (or should I say triple career) to help them and their families invest.

Dominic Vricella, Scott Clarke, Mike Sawyer, Denis White, Lou and Fran Palena, Joyce Patterson Madrid Terri, Arthur Folks, Vince McCalla, Randy Smith, Joe Dino, Brian Fortney, Keisha Porter, Mike Chuppe, Rob Schoenfelder, Mike Dinaso, Roberto Mangual, Clyde Bland, Eric DiValerio, Joe Peretta, Joe Cerini, Joey Clidy, Wayne Matthews, Ralph Ivey, Reggie Goring, Mark Cunard, Scott Bagby, Jason Adams, Glen McCourt, Mark Welhelm, Jason Jenkins, Robert Ekins, Johnny Rodriguez, Marco Rodriguez, Bob Caruso, Rocco Gallelli, Fernandez Massenberg, Jimmy Conley, Anthony Pacificio, and Vonnie Waters.

Also a special thanks to my real estate partners, Calvin and Elaine Clidy. Mom, I want to thank you for all you have done for me. All those practices and games, you made them all. You have always been my #1 Fan! Love you.

About the Author

John Clidy comes from the heart of working-class America. From the time he was old enough to swing a hammer, he worked with his dad in the family roofing business, returning during the summertime and school breaks as he pursued his education.

Hot roofing is a physically demanding job. Add in the fact that many of John's co-workers were convicted felons given a second chance after serving time, it's easy to see how life-experience molded the young man.

This was no union job with guaranteed benefits and money. This was hard-labor employment. John learned about hard work and hard knocks on the sunbaked, tar-topped roofs of New Jersey homes. Reflecting on those days, John says,

"The lessons were clear to me. I learned exactly what I did not want to do. Unfortunately, I learned another lesson in college: that I was not going to play professional football. After two season-ending surgeries, it became clear that I must develop a great career, one that did not depend on athletic prowess."

Today, John Clidy wears many business hats.

- Operating Principal of Keller Williams Realty Washington Township. He opened the office in 2012 and has expanded from starting his sales team of six agents to nearly 400 agents.
- Regional Director of the Greater PA Region which covers three states (NJ, PA, DE) and consists of nearly 10,000 agents in 49 market centers.
- Investor in five other market centers inside the region.
- Investor who runs the Clidy Group, the home of his real estate team.

The Clidy Group began in 1999. John's award-winning real estate team has sold 3,000 plus units and achieved more than $400 million dollars in sold sales volume since inception.

As a real estate investor, John has flipped over 100 homes and holds over $7 million in real estate assets.

Real estate wasn't his only career. John Clidy retired as a Detective Sergeant from the New Jersey State Police, having given 17 years of service. He walked away, three years shy of vesting a pension for life to pursue his dream. Today his KW profit share has surpassed his pension!!

As the author of this book, John achieves another aspect of his dream: using his story to help others live a life by design.

"Go after your dreams if you want to be successful and 100% happy with your life."

LEAVING 6 FIGURES

Monthly Budget

PROJECTED MONTHLY INCOME	Income 1	$0
	Extra income	$0
	Total monthly income	**$0**

ACTUAL MONTHLY INCOME	Income 1	$0
	Extra income	$0
	Total monthly income	**$0**

PROJECTED BALANCE (Projected income minus expenses)	**$0**
ACTUAL BALANCE (Actual income minus expenses)	**$0**
DIFFERENCE (Actual minus projected)	**$0**

HOUSING	Projected Cost	Actual Cost	Difference
Mortgage or rent	$0		$0
Phone	$0		$0
Electricity	$0		$0
Gas	$0		$0
Water and sewer	$0		$0
Cable	$0		$0
Waste removal	$0		$0
Maintenance or repairs	$0		$0
Supplies	$0		$0
Cell Phone	$0		$0
Subtotals	$0	$0	$0

TRANSPORTATION	Projected Cost	Actual Cost	Difference
Vehicle payment	$0		$0
Bus/taxi fare			$0
Insurance	$0		$0
Licensing	$0		$0
Fuel	$0		$0
Parking/Tolls	$0		$0
Maintenance			$0
Other			$0
Subtotals	$0	$0	$0

INSURANCE	Projected Cost	Actual Cost	Difference
Home	$0		$0
Health	$0		$0
Life	$0		$0
Medical/Dental			$0
Prescription Drugs	$0		$0
Long Term Care	$0		$0
Disability	$0		$0
Other			$0
Subtotals	$0	$0	$0

FOOD	Projected Cost	Actual Cost	Difference
Groceries	$0		$0
Dining out	$0		$0
Other			$0
Subtotals	$0	$0	$0

PETS	Projected Cost	Actual Cost	Difference
Food	$0		$0
Medical	$0		$0
Grooming	$0		$0
Toys			$0
Other			$0
Subtotals	$0	$0	$0

PERSONAL CARE	Projected Cost	Actual Cost	Difference
Medical	$0		$0
Hair/nails	$0		$0
Clothing	$0		$0
Dry cleaning	$0		$0
Health club	$0		$0
Organization dues or fees	$0		$0
Education	$0		$0
Subtotals	$0	$0	$0

ENTERTAINMENT	Projected Cost	Actual Cost	Difference
Video/DVD	$0		$0
CDs	$0		$0
Movies	$0		$0
Concerts	$0		$0
Sporting events	$0		$0
Live theater	$0		$0
Vacation	$0		$0
Recreation	$0		$0
Hobbies	$0		$0
Kids Sports	$0		$0
Other	$0		$0
Subtotals	$0	$0	$0

LOANS	Projected Cost	Actual Cost	Difference
Personal			$0
Student			$0
Loan Payments	$0		$0
Credit card	$0		$0
Credit card			$0
Bank Charges			$0
Other			$0
Subtotals	$0	$0	$0

TAXES	Projected Cost	Actual Cost	Difference
Federal	$0	$0	$0
State	$0	$0	$0
Property Taxes			
Local			$0
Other			$0
Subtotals	$0	$0	$0

SAVINGS OR INVESTMENTS	Projected Cost	Actual Cost	Difference
Retirement account	$0	$0	$0
Investment account	$0	$0	$0
Other			$0
Subtotals	$0	$0	$0

GIFTS AND DONATIONS	Projected Cost	Actual Cost	Difference
Gifts	$0		$0
Charity 1			$0
Charity 2			$0
Charity 3			$0
Subtotals	$0	$0	$0

LEGAL	Projected Cost	Actual Cost	Difference
Attorney			$0
Alimony			$0
Child Support			$0
Payments on lien or judgment			$0
Other			$0
Subtotals	$0	$0	$0

Home Care	Projected Cost	Actual Cost	Difference
Domestic Help	$0		$0
Dependent Help	$0		$0
Child Care			$0
Payments on lien or judgment			$0
Allowances			$0
Subtotals	$0	$0	$0

TOTAL PROJECTED COST	**$0**
TOTAL ACTUAL COST	**$0**
TOTAL DIFFERENCE	**$0**

Download available on www.leaving6figures.com

The Leaving 6 Figures Job Declaration

I DECLARE…

I will leave my current job as:

....

and pursue the career I've been waiting for by:

....

(Date)

....

....

Signature / Date   Signature / Date

Witnessed by one who loves me,

Made in the USA
Middletown, DE
22 March 2022

63002187R00109